Callie felt a stampede of butterflies invade her stomach as the woman's dark eyes again captured her.

"Take your clothes off and I'll find you a blanket to wrap up in," Givens said, holding Callie's gaze for another moment before going to the nearby bed and removing a blanket.

Callie struggled to control her breathing and fumbled with her shirt buttons, but her fingers seemed to have forgotten how to act.

"You're freezing. Let me help." Dr. Givens folded the blanket over her own shoulder and slowly began to unbutton Callie's shirt. Unable to meet those haunting dark eyes again, Callie focused her attention on the bright patterns on the blanket. She heard her own sharp intake of breath as Dr. Givens' fingertips gently brushed against the bare skin of her stomach.

A thousand thoughts ran through Callie's mind, but none of them lingered long enough for her to grasp. All she could do was stand there in a daze as the woman eased the sopping shirt back off Callie's shoulders.

"You're very beautiful," she murmured as her hands trailed down Callie's back, pushing away the wet shirt.

LADY BE GOOD

Erotic Love Stories by
Naiad Press Authors

Edited by **Barbara Grier**
and **Christine Cassidy**

THE NAIAD PRESS, INC.
1997

Printed in the United States of America on acid-free paper
First Edition

Cover designer: Bonnie Liss (Phoenix Graphics)
Typesetter: Sandi Stancil

Library of Congress Cataloging-in-Publication Data

Lady be good : erotic love stories by Naiad Press authors / edited by Barbara Grier and Christine Cassidy.
   p.   cm.
   ISBN 1-56280-180-5
   1. Lesbians—Sexual behavior—Fiction. 2. Erotic stories, American. I. Grier, Barbara. II. Cassidy, Christine. III. Naiad Press (Firm)
PS648.L47L34   1997
813'.01083538'086643—dc21   97-10802
                                            CIP

ABOUT THE EDITORS

Barbara Grier

Author, editor, bibliographer, writings include *The Lesbian in Literature, Lesbiana, The Lesbian's Home Journal, Lavender Herring, Lesbian Lives* as well as contributions to various anthologies, *The Lesbian Path* (Cruikshank) and *The Coming Out Stories* (Stanley and Wolfe). She is co-editor, with Katherine V. Forrest, of *The Erotic Naiad* (1992), *The Romantic Naiad* (1993), *The Mysterious Naiad* (1994). She co-edited *The First Time Ever* (1995) and *Dancing in the Dark* (1996)with Christine Cassidy.

Her early career included working for sixteen years with the pioneer lesbian magazine *The Ladder.* For the last twenty-five years she has been, together with Donna J. McBride, the guiding force behind THE NAIAD PRESS.

Articles about Barbara's and Donna's life are too numerous to list, but a good early overview can be found in *Heartwoman* by Sandy Boucher (N.Y., Harper, 1982).

She lives in Tallahassee, Florida.

Christine Cassidy

Christine Cassidy is the Director of Marketing and Circulation at Poets & Writers, Inc., a contributing editor to the *Lambda Book Report* and an editor for the Naiad Press since 1988. A poet, she is the recipient of a New Jersey State Council on the Arts grant in poetry. She also writes reviews, essays, articles and stories, and has been published in *The Persistent Desire: A Femme/Butch Reader,*

The Lambda Book Report, Our World, Poets & Writers Magazine, and *On Our Backs,* among others. She can be seen, courtesy of photographer Morgan Gwenwald, in *Butch/Femme,* a lively collection of photos edited by MG Soares. She lives in New York City.

CONTENTS

Lay Lady Lay

Laura Adams

Her hair was scented with apricot, and her ivory limbs entwined me. There was no mistaking her intentions as her rose-tinted lips parted, inviting a kiss of sweet promise. My crooning whimper of need made her laugh softly against my mouth, then she laid down on the bed, pulling me on top of her.

Then she lay down on the bed . . .

Then she lied . . .

I would never forgive my ex for taking all of the

1

writing guides with her. My at-work library wasn't up to a finer point of grammar.

My crooning whimper of need made her laugh softly against my mouth, then she pulled me into her arms and we tumbled onto the bed.

With the tips of her fingers on my back, she invited my kiss. I put all my desire for her into my exploration of her mouth. We'd been moving toward this moment for months, and the passion of her response didn't surprise me. The kiss went on and on, tasting and swimming, and rolling over, and then our hands were slipping under shirts, both of us too eager to wait. The sight of her pale beauty in the soft light made me dizzy. The next thing I knew I was lying my head on her stomach.

The next thing I knew I was laying ... I laid ...

Dagnabbit. A teacher had once told me it would be helpful to remember the saying, "Let sleeping dogs lie." Except I could never remember if that was an example of incorrect usage and it was supposed to be "Let sleeping dogs lay."

The next thing I knew my head was on her stomach, and I was breathing in the fragrance of fabric softener from her jeans. A faint hint of leather clung to her shirt from the jacket she admitted she'd bought to impress me. The combination made me even dizzier. She pulled my head to her shoulder, rocking me gently. She whispered something sweet and soothing in my ear, and her gentleness quieted my fears. The dizziness receded. We lay that way for several minutes ...

Is it the lie of the land and lay down beside me? Have letters been laying on the table or does your body lie comfortably at night? It has something to do with animals lying and people laying . . . or is it the other way around? Because people lie and animals don't. Except for cats, who will look right at you and claim no knowledge of how the bag of Meow Mix on top of the refrigerator ended up on the kitchen floor.

We breathed in unison for a few minutes, then she took my hand and placed it on her breast. She whispered that she had longed for my touch from the moment I moved into the cubicle next to hers. She had laid in her bed, night after night . . .

I know that you lay flattery on with a trowel, and say, "Now I lay me down to sleep," but had I lain with my ex? I had gotten laid, that's for sure, and in the end been screwed.

She had tossed and turned, night after night, thinking of my hands, my hips, my thighs. Her breast was warm under my palm, and I told her she had walked in my daydreams. She said I was a sweet talker, and her soft voice caressed my ears. I flushed and licked my lips, aware of my rising fever. I wanted to lie my soul bare to her intimate gaze . . .

Lay my soul bare? We lay down arms, and lay in each other's arms. Or do we lie in each other's arms whilst the wolf lays down with the lamb?

I wanted to open my soul to her intimate gaze, to know her, to breathe her in. I wanted to flood my body with her essence. Listening for months to her low voice on the phone, brushing past her in the hall, enduring the scream of my libido — it made this moment of touching too long, and yet I prolonged it, knowing that when touching turned to stroking, the moment of wanting would be gone forever. Stroking would lead to nuzzling and lying my head on her thigh.

I know that strange women lying in ponds are not a good basis for a system of government, but what if they are laying in the street, or if the responsibility of government is laid at their doorstep?

Stroking would lead to nuzzling, and nuzzling to drinking at the well of her passion. I moaned her name as I inhaled her perfume, treasuring the anticipation. Then my mouth sank into her and she lay back on the pillows . . .

A shadow had fallen across my screen, and I hastily turned it off, knowing it was too late. I prayed it wasn't my boss. Then the shadow-maker leaned over my shoulder and turned the screen back on. She smelled of apricots and fabric softener, and just a hint of leather.

Her breast was hard into my shoulder as she scrolled slowly through all that I had written. I swallowed hard, squirming with embarrassment and anticipating her shocked outrage.

Her voice in my ear had the goosebump-inducing, desire-flaming, heartbeat-racing effect I'd known it would.

She whispered, "A chicken laid an egg. The llama lies down. The lovers went home and lay down on their big brass bed. Does that help?"

I shook my head.

"If you'd like to have dinner at my place, I could demonstrate."

I screwed up all my courage and looked up at her. She was laughing at me. I managed to weakly echo, "Demonstrate?"

"Of course I'm not a chicken, nor am I a llama."
Which left . . . I swallowed.

"I'm not kidding about the big brass bed. Care to
lay on it?"

I nodded. Enthusiastically.

A Kiss Is Just A Kiss

Lyn Denison

Meggy was coming home after four very long years. During that time I always seemed to be away when she visited her family. But I never forgot her.

I was eight years old when I met Meggy and she was a very grown-up almost twelve-year-old. From the first moment I set eyes on her I knew she was the most beautiful girl I'd ever seen in my entire life.

But perhaps I should start at the beginning. When I was eight my family moved from an isolated cane farm back to town to live in the big old colonial home where my father had grown up. It was the summer school vacation so, being kids, we gravitated to the large park at the end of the street.

I was swinging upside down on the climbing frame when a voice nearly scared me half to death.

"I wish I could do that."

I regained my hold and glared at the fair-haired boy who stood watching me. "It's easy," I said with feigned nonchalance and swung down so I could get a look at him right side up.

"Easy for you maybe," the boy said with a rueful grin, "but I get all dizzy."

He was about my own age and he followed me when I walked over to the swings. I sat on one and he lowered himself onto the other.

"I'm Mike. Mike Dunleavy. I live down the road from you. What's your name?"

I hesitated. He looked all right but you never could tell with boys. I glanced over to check that my brothers were nearby. "Lexie Rowan," I said reluctantly, and he held out his hand.

"Pleased to meet you, Lexie."

And then someone called his name.

Mike and I turned around and there stood the most beautiful girl I'd ever seen. She wore faded cut-off jeans and a bright pink T-shirt and she had breasts. I noticed that right away. Her hair was fair and curled about her face and her eyes were very blue.

I just stood there and gaped at her, something I did from that moment on whenever I saw her. Of course, as time went by I learned to disguise it but, believe me, inside me I gaped at her.

"Lexie, this is my sister, Meggy," Mike was saying.

His sister. Good grief! How I wished I had a sister like Meggy. Then as the years passed I was very grateful Meggy Dunleavy and I weren't blood relations but I managed to hide that fact, too, until that night. But I'm getting ahead of myself.

From that day in the park Mike and I became firm friends. Going to the new school after the holidays was easier because he was in my class and because Meggy walked us to school.

My brothers teased me mercilessly about my boyfriend, Mike. For the most part I took it goodnaturedly. I mean, who wouldn't want to have a boyfriend who had a sister as beautiful as Meggy?

My mother smiled fondly on my friendship with Mike, until we went to the first-term dance together when we were fourteen. That elicited a motherdaughter talk about the things nice girls didn't do with boys which, needless to say, set me thinking about just that. So I kissed Mike to see what it was like.

Well, that's kind of stretching the truth a little. What really happened was, I was thinking these licentious thoughts and suddenly I saw myself kissing Meggy. I nearly had a heart attack and the shock drove me to kiss Mike. And it wasn't just to see what it was like. It was to prove to myself I'd like kissing boys and that the wonderful, exciting, exhilarating feelings I got when I thought of kissing Mike's sister were just some silly adolescent fantasy.

Huh! What a wonderful piece of self-delusion that was. That kiss Mike and I shared was a total nonevent for both of us, and thankfully we laughed about it and went back to being friends. And it didn't stop my daydreaming about Meggy's perfect lips.

When Meggy left home I was desolate. She joined the Navy and went down South to do her training. I missed her like crazy and wrote a hundred letters to her I never posted. I couldn't wait until she came home on leave and I'd hang on every word of her stories about her training, her job. Then she'd leave again and I'd torture myself with the thought that she had a new life that didn't include me.

I scarcely gave my approaching sixteenth birthday a thought. If I hadn't been moping over Meggy's absence I probably would have noticed that no one else mentioned my upcoming birthday either, which was suspicious, as birthdays were special in our family. All the while my parents were plotting a surprise party for me. It was an absolute success. I was genuinely, positively taken by surprise.

Meggy was coming too but her plane had been delayed and I was in a fever of indecisive anticipation. I'd had a few glasses of wine my mother missed seeing, and I was sort of glowing by the time Meggy walked in at eleven o'clock.

She'd come straight from the airport and was still dressed in her uniform. I wouldn't have believed she could be more beautiful, but she was that night.

"Happy birthday, Lexie," she said with a smile.

Her gaze moved over me and I grew even hotter, as though she'd actually touched me. She handed me a small box wrapped in silver paper and festooned with curling red ribbons.

My hands were shaking so much I couldn't get the gift unwrapped and she laughingly took it back, dispensing with the paper, handing me a velvet jeweler's box. Inside, nestled on white satin, was a pair of tiny gold earrings, hearts set with sapphires.

I removed the earrings I was wearing and fumbled to replace them with Meggy's. She had to help me again and I flushed, wanting to turn my head just slightly, put my lips to her hand as her fingers adjusted the clip on the back of the studs. When the earrings were in place she stood back to admire them.

"They look great," she said with satisfaction.

I touched one small earring. "They're fantastic," I said breathily, and before I could stop myself I stepped forward and put my hands on her arms. All my senses magnified and I breathed in the intoxicating scent that was Meggy, her perfumed soap, her shampoo, the light makeup she wore.

I pressed my cheek to hers and my sense of touch took over. Her skin was like satin and I should have pulled away right then. But instead I moved my head and my lips found hers.

I didn't consciously intend for it to go that far but I was way out of control now, heady with her nearness. As my lips found the softness of hers I heard myself moan softly in my throat and of their own accord my lips opened and my tongue-tip flicked out, caressed the moistness of her mouth.

For one split-second that seemed like a century we stood like that and then Meggy stepped shakily away. Her eyes, dark glistening pools, held mine for one long moment, and then she seemed to draw herself together and turned away to talk to someone else. I hurriedly did the same, part of me totally mortified at my daring, the other part soaring with the wonder of the knowledge that I had finally realized my dream. I'd kissed Meggy Dunleavy.

Of course, in the cold hard light of day my mortification took the upper hand. I was consumed by the worst humiliation I'd ever suffered in my life.

Meggy came over next morning with her family to help clear up after the party but we were never alone together, a fact I was sure Meggy maneuvered, and she left again without either of us mentioning that earth-shattering moment.

That was four years ago. And now Meggy was coming home for another party, her parents' twenty-fifth wedding anniversary.

I was a bundle of nerves as I slipped my one and only party dress over my head. I was about average height, far too thin for my liking, and with my twenty-first birthday in sight I was still waiting for my breasts to develop. My brothers called my boobs "a couple of fried eggs" and I couldn't deny they were right.

I picked up the velvet box containing the earrings Meggy had given me and once again it took me ages to steady my hands enough to fix the tiny studs in place.

The Rowans and the Dunleavys were notorious for their backyard parties, and this was no exception. I began mingling with mutual family and friends but I was tingling, my antennae alert for Meggy.

And there she was. She wore a pair of Garbo

pants in some sort of slinky material, a deep rich blue color, and her white sleeveless top fell softly over her breasts. She was still the most beautiful woman I'd ever seen in my life.

Just then she looked up and right at me and a shaft of pure desire shot through me. I was amazed no one else was aware of the sparks of electricity that darted about the air between us. But maybe it was only my hopeful imagination. Why would Meggy Dunleavy — and if what Mike told me this afternoon was true, the soon-to-be-engaged Meggy Dunleavy — have any feelings for me?

Meggy began crossing the patio toward me and with every step she took I became more breathless.

"Hello, Lexie. It must be years since we've seen each other."

"Hi! And yes, I guess it is."

"You've changed a little."

"Not me. I'm always the same."

"Well, you've definitely grown up."

"I hope so. I'm nudging twenty-one."

Meggy smiled ruefully. "We're all getting on."

We wandered inside to refill our wine glasses. I wanted to gulp mine down but when I took a sedate sip I could scarcely swallow it.

But Meggy was saying something about photographs, of the base where she was stationed, where she lived, and would I like to see them? I followed her upstairs to her room.

I'd been in this room on any number of occasions over the years but tonight I wanted to hang back. And race madly inside.

"It looks the same," I said inanely as Meggy switched on the lamp by her bed.

"What does?" she asked, and I could have sworn there was a catch in her voice.

"Your room."

"Oh." Meggy cleared her throat. "That's one of the things I like about coming home. The familiarity of my room." She looked across at me and my own throat closed again.

My nerve endings were stretched to the breaking point. How I wished I had the courage to simply walk over to her, take her in my arms.

She wasn't wearing a ring but I had to ask the question that had been on my mind all afternoon.

"Mike said you're getting engaged," I made myself say.

"Did he?" Meggy leaned back against the window sill and took a sip of her wine. "Mum and Dad are hoping."

I couldn't for the life of me say a word.

Meggy continued to give the wine in her glass a thorough examination and then she sighed. "Brian's asked me to consider the possibility."

A stillness stretched between us.

"And are you?" I felt like I'd swallowed knives. Why didn't I just pour boiling water over myself? Or flay myself with barbed wire?

"Am I considering it?" Meggy shrugged and looked up. "The fact remains I'm getting a little too old to dither, wouldn't you say?"

"You're only twenty-four. That's not old," I said desperately and Meggy laughed softly.

"Your brother, Ross, is not much older than I am and he's married and they're expecting their second child."

I tried for a theatrical gasp and put my hand on my chest. "You mean Ross broke your heart by marrying An Other?"

Meggy's laugh played over me. "I love your sense of humor, Lexie. You know you had it when you were just a little kid."

"My saving grace." I wanted to tell her that right now it was hiding a long-standing pain. "So, are you carrying a torch for Ross?"

Meggy paused. "No," she said at last. "Not for Ross."

Who then? I wanted to ask, but by now I'd used up my store of courage.

"So do you have a particular boyfriend?" Meggy asked off-handedly. "Or are you playing the field?"

The question took me by surprise. "I date occasionally." What a laugh. I'd been out with four guys but I wanted to tell her none of them held a candle to her.

"No one special then?" Meggy was gazing casually into her wine glass again.

"No."

"Me, neither."

I thought I'd imagined those two wonderful words. "But what about Brian?" I heard myself say and wondered if I had a problem with self-torture. "Haven't you been going out with him for over a year?"

"On and off."

I took a breath. "Well, don't marry him if he's not the right one." Now I was starting to sound like *Dear Abby*.

Meggy grimaced. "Oh, he's not the right one, I'm afraid," she said softly.

And something in the tension made my heart rate increase triple-fold.

"Do you remember your sixteenth birthday party?" Meggy asked and my mouth went dry.

Did I remember it? It was etched indelibly in my brain.

"I remember it vividly," Meggy continued. "My plane was held up and I thought I was going to miss your party."

I had to say something. I opened my mouth but nothing ventured forth. Where was my wonderful sense of humor when I really needed it?

"Everyone was in the back yard, much like tonight, only it was three doors down at your place. You were wearing a shimmery blue dress."

She'd looked wonderful in her Naval uniform.

"I must admit it took me aback for a moment. I hadn't seen you for months and suddenly you seemed, well, you weren't a little kid any longer."

I made myself laugh. "I thought I was very adult."

The room seemed to vibrate with the silence until Meggy spoke again. "You're wearing my earrings tonight."

"I like them." I swallowed and shakily touched my earlobes.

"I had to help you open the box," Meggy said huskily, and her voice poured over me like warm, liquid honey. "And then . . ." She paused and I cringed.

Did she remember?

Meggy looked up and her eyes sparkled in the lamp-lit room. "Then you kissed me."

"Must have been the wine." I struggled to keep my voice even. "I wasn't used to it and, well, I just wanted to thank you for the gift," I finished lamely.

Meggy's lips twisted. "Do you usually kiss other women like that?"

I tried for the safety of humor again and rolled my eyes. "Oh, all the time." I forced a laugh. "I thought you might have forgotten. It was just a kiss."

"Just a kiss?" Meggy's blue eyes burned into mine and I felt the tension shift again, escalate, if that was possible. "No, I didn't forget that kiss, Lexie. I tried to. In the beginning I tried to tell myself I'd imagined it. The way it felt. The way I felt. I kept away. I didn't want to see you, to —"

"Look, Meggy, I'm sorry. I didn't mean for it to cause you any grief. I just, well, it was just —"

"Just a kiss." She smiled crookedly. "You said that. That kiss was —" She made a small movement with one hand. "I finally figured it out. And I want to thank you, Lexie."

"For what?" I asked hoarsely.

Meggy shrugged. "For showing me the light. For saving my life. I'd tried for years to work out what was wrong with me. I knew some great guys but none of them did anything for me. It was all such a charade, a sham."

My chest hurt. What was she saying?

"So I went along to some women's bars. That

sounds so easy but it wasn't. It took me ages to pluck up my courage to go, but it saved my sanity. It really did. I've met lots of wonderful women. So thank you, Lexie."

My glow of hope crashed into a thousand shards, each one cutting into me like saber thrusts. "Did you? I mean, is there a special woman then?"

"Yes, I think so."

"Oh." I'd never felt so miserable in my life. I had to get away. There was only so much I could take. "Look, I'd better be getting back to the party." I took hold of the door knob. "Everyone will be wondering where we are."

Meggy pushed herself away from the windowsill and in two steps was standing within inches of me. She put her hand on the door and closed it again. Then she reached out, ran her hand lightly down my bare arm, and I froze.

"I like your hair like this," she said slowly. Her finger flicked at a strand of my hair and then settled on my cheek. I burned where she touched me. "About that kiss..."

I felt so hot I thought I'd ignite. I had to be dreaming this. Then her soft lips touched mine, lips as silky as crushed velvet. And kissing Meggy was just as wonderful as I'd remembered.

She went to move away but I found my motor skills and I reached up, slid my fingers in her hair and kissed her with all the welled-up wanting of years. When we broke apart we were both breathless.

"God, Lexie." Meggy groaned, inciting me, and my knees nearly gave way beneath me. Her breath teased my skin and I melted into her.

My hands moved under her blouse, felt the cool skin of her back, my fingertips playing over the indentation of her spine. Then I slid one hand around to her midriff, moved upwards and cupped the soft mound of her full breast.

She plucked at the zipper at the back of my dress and the sound of it sliding down echoed around us and we both paused, looked at each other.

"Do you want me to stop?" Meggy asked thickly, and I gave a soft laugh.

"Don't you dare. It's taken me a dozen years to get to this place and I'm not going back."

She chuckled and then sobered. "Oh, Lexie," she murmured. I pulled her blouse over her head, unclipped her bra and dispensed with her trousers. I'd dreamed of this moment for so long.

Then we were on her bed and our hot skin merged. We kissed and caressed each other with feverish abandonment. My lips slid down over her smooth skin and I murmured deep in my throat, my voice so low and aroused I scarcely recognized it.

Her mouth found my small nipples and I arched in an ache of desire. Her fingers were caressing me lightly, across my abdomen, encircling my navel, darting lower, teasing me unmercifully.

"Please, Meggy," I heard myself beg, and then she was slipping her fingers down through my damp, dark curls and sliding inside me. "Don't stop," I encouraged, moving against her, and she gave a low laugh.

"Not now, Lexie. Not ever."

And then I was cascading all over her and she muffled my cry with her mouth on mine. My heart was thundering inside me, beating a reckless tattoo. When I caught my breath she was looking down at me with those beautiful blue eyes.

I smiled crookedly. "I've been in love with you since I was eight years old," I said, and she shook her head.

"What took you so long to tell me?"

"I tried to tell you. With that kiss."

"While I tried to tell myself that that kiss was just a kiss." Meggy shook her head slightly. "I've kissed a few women since that night, Lexie, but it was never the same. Finally I acknowledged what I knew all along, that I had to come back to you, take the chance that it wasn't just a kiss."

"To quote you, what took you so long?"

She laughed and touched my lips gently with her finger. "I'm such a slow learner I think you'd better kiss me again, don't you?"

And I did.

Unladylike Behavior
Kate Calloway

I was out in front shooting baskets with Deano and Ricky and showing off something fierce. I was trying to teach them what I called the Karen Kennedy Special. I dribbled with my left hand out past the free-throw line, did a quick behind-the-back roll and lobbed a right-handed hook shot right through the net.

Deano spit on the cement. "Damn, Karen. You shoot better'n a boy."

"Better'n you, that's for sure," Ricky said, his

braces gleaming at his brother. "Show me that behind-the-back thingie again." At thirteen, he was a year younger than Deano and me, but he was a better shot than his older brother. Of my three cousins, Ricky was my favorite. Not just because we looked alike with our blond hair and blue eyes but because we shared a sometimes perverse sense of humor.

"The trick is, you gotta start using your left hand, boys. You're limiting yourselves by insisting on dribbling with your right." I demonstrated the move again and watched with satisfaction as the ball whooshed through, barely kissing the net.

"Karen! Grandma Kay is looking for you! She wants to curl your hair!" Missy, my youngest cousin came prancing out of the house, her own blond hair done up in pink ribbons. Missy was eleven going on twenty-one. One look told me she and Grandma Kay had been into Aunt Leah's makeup again.

"Uh, could you tell her you couldn't find me?" I said, making a jump shot from behind the free-throw line. I followed this with a left-handed lay-up.

"But she knows you're out here. She's says it's time for you to come in." Missy stood with her hands on her hips and dared me to challenge her. She may have looked like Shirley Temple, but she had Attila the Hun's blood running right through her.

Groaning, I tossed the ball to Ricky and followed Missy inside. The last thing I wanted was to have Grandma Kay start fussing with my hair. But she was the only grandmother I had. And besides, she got such a kick out of it, how could I deny her?

"Karen, there you are. Why, you're dirty as an old

mud hen! Go wash those hands and then come sit right over here. I want to do something with that hair of yours." Grandma Kay was just under five feet tall, but her recently bleached bouffant do added a couple of inches.

I took a quick peek at the dressing table. No scissors, thank God. I washed my hands and reluctantly sat on the velvet cushion, facing myself in the mirror.

"I sure would like to see you start parting your hair on the side," she said, running a comb through my blond tangles.

"I like it this way," I tried, knowing it was no use. Once I was trapped on the velvet cushion, Grandma Kay wasn't about to let me up until she'd done a complete makeover. I closed my eyes and tried to bear it with good humor.

That was the summer that my mother got sick and they had to ship me off to stay with my cousins in Mapleton, the armpit of the West. Grandma Kay was ecstatic, of course, having another girl to fuss over, and my aunt and uncle looked at it as an extra pair of hands to help with the farm chores. Ricky and Deano were genuinely thrilled to have me for the whole summer but Missy seemed to resent my presence. At first she'd been as excited as her older brothers, but once she realized she was no longer the center of attention, she started to shoot me devilish black looks across the dinner table. I tried to shrug it off. It was only for a little while, I told myself. I could endure Missy's jealousy, Grandma Kay's curlers and even the drudgery of living in a tiny, dirt encrusted town for two months. But in my heart, I couldn't wait for the summer to end. That is, until I met Inky Madison.

We were at dinner that night when my Aunt Leah broke the bad news. Right after Uncle Dean had offered grace and I was about to dig into the mashed potatoes that accompanied nearly every meal, she dropped the bomb.

"Good news, Karen. Tomorrow, you and Missy are going to begin your first day of finishing school!"

I'm afraid I choked on my potatoes and nearly had to excuse myself from the table. Deano was chuckling behind his napkin, but Ricky looked at me with pure sympathy.

"What?" I finally managed. They had a rule in that house that no one could be excused from the table until everyone had cleaned their plate. I learned on the very first night to take tiny portions, but even so, I looked at the food congealing on the chipped stoneware in front of me and felt nauseous. My appetite had vanished.

"Miss Nation's Girls Academy!" Missy chirped. Her dark eyes brimmed over with excitement. "I've been begging to go for years!"

"Most girls don't go until twelve, but Missy's ready, and we think you are too. It's a gift from your grandmother. Right after dinner, you should call and thank her." Grandma Kay lived just a block away but only ate dinner with us on the weekends. I didn't know if it was because she preferred her own cooking or whether it was because Uncle Dean refused to let her have a glass of wine with dinner, but either way, I didn't blame her.

"What exactly," I asked, trying to regain my composure, "is finishing school?" I'd heard of it, of course. But it seemed like something out of a bad movie. Something they probably only still did in hick places like Mapleton.

"People save up a long time for the privilege of sending their daughters to Miss Nation's," my uncle intoned. He was a tall, bony man with hard, chiseled features. He carried a Bible with him, even to the dinner table. He rarely smiled and never laughed. Thank God my cousins all took after Aunt Leah. I couldn't imagine spending the whole summer in a house full of Uncle Deans.

"Our people have been sending their daughters to finishing school since our ancestors came over on the *Mayflower*," Aunt Leah explained. Since I'd been there, she'd managed to mention the *Mayflower* nearly every day. They were poor by city standards, but they came from good stock, and God save the person who forgot it. I secretly thanked the Lord that my own father had managed to escape Mapleton and all its small-town idiosyncrasies. He was the complete opposite of his brother, for which I was also eternally grateful, and no one in my family had ever mentioned the *Mayflower* once. Let alone any damn finishing school!

"A girl needs to be properly schooled in the finer points of becoming a lady," Leah went on. "Finishing school just adds the finishing touches. Of course, some girls are farther along than others. But don't you fret. In a few weeks, you'll be right up there with the rest of them."

"A few weeks?" My heart sank down to my knees. Missy beamed at me from across the table and it was all I could do not to kick her in the shin. Obviously, she considered herself to be "farther along" than I was.

The next morning Ricky and Deano stood in the driveway bouncing the basketball between them while I slid into the back seat of the station wagon behind Missy. I'd packed what few clothes I'd brought with me for the summer, mostly shorts and jeans, sneakers and T-shirts. Aunt Leah had insisted on throwing in a couple of her dresses that hung on me and made me feel both frumpy and ridiculous. Naturally, Missy had brought a whole array of pink and yellow dresses and she wore little black patent leather shoes that made me want to stomp on her toes, just once, to sort of tone down the sheen.

I waved disconsolately at my cousins as the station wagon pulled out of the driveway and rambled down the dirt road into town. It was a twenty-mile trek and I grew more miserable with each passing telephone pole. By the time we arrived at Miss Nation's Girls Academy, I was in a truly awesome funk.

"Welcome, ladies! Just bring your things right in. We're so very pleased you could join us!" Miss Nation herself, I presumed, was pushing seventy. But her hair was jet black, compliments of Lady Clairol, and her chins had been lifted at least once. When she took my hand, her skin was cool and dry, like a lizard's. She looked at Missy approvingly and then her gaze fell on me. She couldn't quite stifle the impending frown as she took in my faded Levis, worn tennies and sleeveless sweatshirt. Even Aunt Leah hadn't been able to talk me out of wearing my favorite shirt. "Very well," Miss Nation said, her ruby lips pursed as if accustomed to the formidable challenge that a girl like me posed. "You're just in time for our first ballroom dancing lesson. I'll show you to your rooms and once you've freshened up, you can join the others in the hall."

The first good thing that happened that day was that Missy and I were not roomed together. She'd been placed with another eleven-year-old and I had been assigned a room with the only other fourteen-year-old at the school. I opened the dorm-room door and caught my first glimpse of Inky Madison.

We stared at each other a full minute before breaking into spontaneous grins.

"Well, hot damn!" she said. "I was afraid they'd give me some simpering debutante. You wanna smoke?" She was perched on the dresser beneath the window, her red sneakers swinging freely off the ground. She reached into the top drawer and pulled out a crumpled pack of Pall Malls.

"Uh, we better not." I could still hear Miss Nation's heels clicking down the hallway.

Inky shrugged and stuffed the pack back down into the drawer, then introduced herself. "How come I never seen you around?"

"Visiting my cousins. My grandma thought this might make a lady out of me."

"Lord, I hope not," Inky said, laughing. For the

first time since I'd come to Mapleton, I felt myself relax. I opened my suitcase and started putting things away.

"How'd you get a name like Inky, anyway?"

"My little brother couldn't say Mindy, thank God. Inky suits me much better. Even my mother admits it. Least you got some dresses," she added, hopping down to examine my meager belongings.

"They're my Aunt Leah's. She insisted I bring them. I have no intention of wearing them."

"Good." She picked up my Giants baseball cap and twirled it on her finger. "Cool." She put it on backwards, just the way I liked to wear it, and turned to examine herself in the tiny mirror. She looked good, I thought. Taller than I, Inky had short golden-brown hair cut in layers and dark, laughing eyes. She was lean and muscular with a bounce in her step that somehow matched the crooked grin she wore. I blushed when I realized I was staring. "You got a boyfriend?" she asked, catching me off balance.

"Not really," I said. At fourteen, most of my friends were already going steady, and although they seemed to be on an eternal quest to match me up with someone, I'd thus far managed to avoid the whole dating scene. "Too busy," I added, feeling that I needed to explain. Inky just smiled.

"Yeah? What do you do that keeps you so busy?" She had plopped herself on the edge of my bed and was tossing my baseball cap in the air.

"Oh, you know. Basketball, track. I'm on the newspaper staff at school. And I'm taking guitar lessons. Stuff like that. How about you?"

"Huh?" She suddenly seemed embarrassed.

"You got a boyfriend?"

"Nah. I don't go in for that." She paused. "Too busy," she added, grinning. Just then there was a crackling sound followed by Miss Nation's melodious voice over the intercom.

"Ballroom dancing lessons will begin in ten minutes in the dance hall. All young ladies should report immediately."

"Oh boy, here we go," Inky said.

"I can't believe I have to do this," I concurred.

"Maybe it won't be all bad. At least we can dance together."

"You think so?" My heart did a little flipflop and I felt my cheeks grow warm.

"Sure. We get to pick our own partners. Come on, I'll show you."

With no warning, Inky took me in her arms and twirled me around the tiny dorm room. I'd never danced so close to anyone before, never felt the light-headedness that threatened to send me toppling, and yet I felt secure in Inky's arms and liked the way she moved me around the room. When we stumbled over my suitcase and fell onto the bed, we were both laughing.

"You dance real good," Inky said, peering down at me. She had fallen on top of me and I could feel her heartbeat as she lay pressed against me. Sounds of our breathing filled the room.

"Where'd you learn to dance like that?" I asked, beginning to squirm beneath the weight of her body. She wasn't heavy. It was just that I wasn't sure I liked the way my heart had begun to hammer.

"I've been here before," she said, grinning. "My

folks are bound and determined to make a lady of me. As you can see, it didn't exactly take the first time. Kinda doubt it's gonna take *this* time." Her lips were just inches above mine and her dark eyes bore right through me. I felt short of breath.

"Inky, we should probably get going."

"Yeah, we probably should." She shifted her weight as if to move away and then, to my utter amazement, she leaned down and touched her lips to mine. My stomach dropped to the floor and my heart slammed against my chest. My eyes must have been wide as saucers.

"What'd you do that for?" I managed. For once, she'd lost her grin. Her face had gone serious and I realized with a start that she was the most beautiful girl I'd ever known.

"Oh, Lord," she said. "I sure as hell didn't mean for that to happen." She scrambled off me and stood at the foot of the bed straightening her clothes. Her cheeks were as pink as tulips. "I'm sorry," she stammered looking at me with pleading eyes as I got to my feet.

Surprising myself, I stood and put my hands on her shoulders, pulling her toward me. I had to stand on my toes just a little but my lips found hers and this time my eyes closed while we kissed. It was the first real kiss of my life. The first kiss I wanted. The first one to send my stomach parachuting in a downward spiral while my heart soared skyward. It may have lasted thirty seconds but seemed closer to an hour. When I finally pulled away, Inky's dark eyes were glistening and we were both breathless.

"Just one thing," I said, putting my Giants cap

on her head. "You dance with anyone else, I'm gonna have to kick some serious ass."

"Oh, now, Miss Nation wouldn't stand for that," she said, feigning indignation. "It wouldn't be ladylike behavior." Inky giggled, adjusted the cap and offered me her arm.

As the two of us paraded down the hall toward the dance room I felt a part of me I'd long ignored begin to unfold inside me, spreading like a warm syrup through my veins. I tingled and my whole being hummed. And then, in one of those rare epiphanic moments of truth, a thought so pure and simple came to me that I laughed aloud. Miss Nation may not be able to teach me how to be ladylike, I thought, grinning like a fool, but I had a feeling Inky Madison was going to teach me all about liking ladies.

Waiting for the Rain
Ann O'Leary

The wind caught at her skirt, twisting it around her legs, causing her to stumble. Her oversized man's shirt was billowing, threatening to tear away from her frail body.

"Puss, puss," Claire was calling, but the wind was snatching her words away. She had brought a bowl of food for the old cat, which had recently had more kittens and was holed up under the house. She put the bowl down near the opening, where the boards were missing, and headed around to the front veranda on the other side of the house.

It was completely still there, facing south. But Claire could hear the northerly wind howling around the back. The dusty old blue heeler had been sensibly waiting for her, lying on the doormat. Apart from feeding the cat, Claire had been feeding her few hens, bantams, and had collected two eggs. She had them in her skirt pocket and thought she might have them for lunch. The boards of the veranda creaked as she walked across to the screen door. The dog got off the mat and waited for the door to open. It was very hot already, and her tongue lolled sideways. Claire turned before she went inside and looked out across the paddocks and at the sky. There were still patches of blue here and there to the south and southeast, but the dark clouds were increasing. By tonight, Claire thought, there'd be a storm. There were bush fires around, being propelled by the strong north wind. They were still a long way from Claire, but she could smell a hint of them on the wind. A good rain would put a stop to them.

Ahead of Claire, the dog waddled up the hallway, her claws clicking on the ancient linoleum. She flopped down in her favorite spot, in the doorway of the kitchen. She had a chance there of catching any cross breeze that might come through.

"Out of the way you silly old thing," Claire muttered to the dog, who ignored her. Claire stepped over her and went to the sink to fill the kettle to make a pot of tea. The water ran slowly from the tap; it was gravity fed, and the tank was less than half full. May had always said they'd get an electric pump for the tank, but it was something they'd never gotten around to doing. She thought of May now. She could see her on a day like this, standing out in the front yard looking up at the clouds, her hands on her hips, her strong athletic legs apart. She'd be wearing trousers tucked into her riding boots and a big loose shirt. She'd be calculating when the rain would come and how much there'd be. She'd be right too; she had an instinct for such things.

Claire originally came from a small country town in northern Victoria. As a young girl, she had hopes of becoming a school teacher. But with her father getting killed in the second world war, there wasn't any money for a teachers college in Melbourne. But her school results were good, and she landed a job at the local bank as a teller. "This job will suit you very well, until you get married," her mother had said. It was in the bank that Claire first met May.

It was a cold wet day when May walked in with a check to cash, from Doctor Parsons. She'd sold some eggs and chickens to his wife. It had been a quiet afternoon in the bank, with few customers, and Claire looked up as the bank door opened. May came in and shook her head a little. Her hair was quite short. Drops of rain flew off her brown tousled curls. Her hands were plunged into the pockets of a heavy overcoat, and she was wearing trousers and boots. It was only when she came closer to the counter that Claire could see she was a young woman.

"Sorry about your floor," May had said, and she smiled at Claire with a stunning smile, revealing perfect white teeth. Her dark eyes sparkled.

Claire was entranced for a few moments by the

young woman's raw beauty. She glanced at the
muddy footprints that marked the shiny bank floor
but was absorbed with that smile and those eyes.

After that, quite often, when Claire finished work,
May would be loitering outside, not far away, and
they'd talk for a while. May had stories about her
animals and her family that made Claire laugh and
filled her with wonder. Her life was so different from
Claire's. May was tall and strong, with a well-
proportioned body and muscles as hard as a boy's,
but her voice and her eyes were soft and gentle.
Sometimes when the weather was fine, they'd walk
for a while until they came to the trees where the
bush began, near the edge of town. Sometimes they'd
share a cigarette, which May would bring. When May
laughed, she shook with low throaty giggles and tears
would come to her eyes. People noticed them together
and didn't approve.

"She's not the sort of girl you should be associ-
ating with," her mother had hissed angrily, and the
bank manager was concerned that his employee
should be seen with this girl from across the river.
From the Aboriginal mission.

So Claire and May began to meet in secret on
weekends. They would meet near the old mine deep
in the bush and would explore together. May showed
Claire all kinds of things she'd never seen before and
enchanted her with her knowledge of the birds and
plants.

One day, when they were standing together,
holding hands, completely still, watching a wallaby
drinking at a waterhole, Claire looked at May. A
shaft of light had filtered down through the treetops

and the sun was dancing on her hair. Her skin was chocolate-brown velvet. The planes of her face absorbed the shadows, and her mouth was set in a smile as she concentrated on the wallaby.

Over recent months, Claire had increasingly revolved her life around the times she could be with May. She longed to be with her. She yearned for the next time she could hold May's strong hand in her own. But now as she looked at her, another kind of longing began to grow in her. It was powerful and came from deep within her.

May turned to look at Claire, and her dark eyes absorbed Claire's desire. May and Claire moved instinctively into each other's arms, and their mouths met in a tentative kiss. Claire felt the desire spread like wildfire all though her body and she trembled with the pleasure of it. May moaned and held Claire more tightly against her body. Claire could feel her heart pounding against her breast.

They kissed passionately and deeply, their tongues exploring and tasting. They reveled in this sensation that was new to both of them. They sank to the forest floor, made a soft nest of grass and leaves, and kissed like this until the evening shadows signaled it was time for Claire to go home.

May walked Claire to the edge of the bush, where the houses began. Claire left her reluctantly, after they'd made plans to meet again the next day. As she walked along the darkening road, she constantly looked back and could just see May, blending with, a part of, the shadows of the leaves.

The following day, they met and embraced with a passion even greater than before. It was very hot, and they made their way through the bush to a secluded part of the riverbank. They stripped off their clothes and plunged into the cool water, playing and laughing like children until their bodies entwined. They got out of the water and spread their clothes out on the ground among the tall river grasses under the trees.

Claire longed for May's brown arms around her, and soon she was lying in the dappled light with May's strong body over her, their mouths pressed together.

May said later that she was overwhelmed with Claire's beauty, pale and vulnerable. May wanted to possess her, to be a part of her.

Claire closed her eyes in an agony of desire as May kissed her breasts. May slid down, until her mouth found the wet, mysterious place that was aching for her touch. Claire placed her thighs on May's broad brown shoulders, and she was enveloped in a new world of exquisite pleasure. Soon, her body arched in a peak of ecstasy. She cried out, a wild sound that blended with the sounds of the bush, and in that moment, she was a part of it. She was one with the trees, the leaves, the birds, the lizards scuttling and the flowing river. They made love all day and knew they had to find a way to be together all the time.

One day, not long after this, Claire received a letter from a country solicitor, informing her that a maiden aunt had died and left her a house with forty acres in the western district, a long way away. She hurried to show the letter to May. This would be their chance to be together. Much to the consternation of their families, they immediately decided to go there and live together. They packed their few belongings and traveled down on the train.

The solicitor met them at the station and drove them to the property. He handed Claire the key to the house and left them standing, rather overwhelmed, on the veranda. There they were, Claire thought, a white woman in a floral dress and a black one in a shirt and trousers with wild hair. They were standing, mesmerized by the evening light on the trees and over the paddocks. May was bathed in pink from the setting sun.

They'd bought some food in the town on the way, and May turned to Claire with shining eyes and said, "I'll find some wood for the stove, and we can cook dinner."

Soon the smoke was puffing comfortingly out of the chimney, and they ate their simple meal by candlelight. That was forty-five years ago.

Claire got a job in town to keep them going while they prepared the land for growing vegetables, and they kept poultry for meat and eggs. They used their small savings to buy materials, make repairs and buy an old tray truck. Within two years, while Claire worked in town, May had built up a market for her produce. It was very hard work for May, and as soon as it was possible, Claire left her job and they worked together on their little farm. They were consumed with their love for each other. Their relationship was viewed suspiciously by the locals, and their families kept away, so they lived in a world of their own. No one else mattered anyway, and their love just increased as the years went by.

* * * * *

Claire jumped slightly at the whistle of the kettle. She got up and poured the water into the teapot. While it was drawing, she looked out the window at the eucalyptus trees bending in the wind. She could see the dust blowing up off the dry paddocks. She remembered that she had never ceased to be amazed by May's ability to make or repair anything. Whenever Claire was worried about money or incessant rains that sometimes threatened to wash them away, or hot dry times like this when even the air crackled like paper, May would always smile and put her strong comforting arms around her. "Everything will be all right," May would say. And it always was. The only times that May looked sad were when Claire was cross with her about something, and it was always something trivial. It never lasted long because Claire couldn't bear to see May's eyes downcast.

Claire took her mug of tea back out onto the front veranda. The dog stayed where she was, causing Claire to have to clamber over her again. Claire sat down in an old wicker chair and looked again at the sky. The rain clouds seemed to have blown away a bit, but the sky looked murky and gray. She could smell smoke more strongly now. She sipped her tea. May would have known what was going to happen and what they should do.

It was a day like this one, three years ago, when May said she'd go and have a look at the shed roof. A sheet of iron had come loose in the wind and was in danger of flying off. They'd just finished lunch, but May had hardly eaten anything. She said she didn't feel well. This was unusual, and Claire had been worried about her. She said she would go and see to the roof, but May stubbornly insisted on doing it herself. In these later years, some jobs had begun to be difficult for them, but May often over-exerted herself.

So May had gone out in the hot wind, and was gone for a long time. Claire thought she must be doing something else as well, and she kept listening for the banging of nails. Eventually she went outside to see what was keeping May. The wind was strong and pushed against her as she walked across the dry spiky yellow grass toward the shed. The dog was down there, and ran out toward her, barking and jumping around excitedly. Claire was calling out to May, but the sound was carried off by the wind. When she got around to the back of the shed, she found May lying in the grass. She'd dragged the ladder out of the shed, but hadn't got as far as standing it up against the wall. Claire fell on her, crying, kissing, shaking her, begging her to wake up. But it was useless. May was dead. A heart attack, the doctor said when he came.

So now, there was just Claire with the old dog, a few chooks and the cat. People said she should go, that she was too old to stay out there on her own. But Claire would never leave. May was here. They'd been together for forty-two years. Claire could see May in the shadows of trees. She could hear her voice on the wind, and in her sleep, she could feel May's strong arms around her and her sweet breath on her face. Claire still ached with love for her, and here, she was still with her.

The empty mug hit the veranda boards with a

clunk. It had fallen out of Claire's hand and rolled off her lap. She must have nodded off for a moment. She looked at the sky again and sniffed the wind. There was still time for the wind to turn around and for the rain to come. She would wait. Regardless of anything, she would stay, where she belonged. With May.

Claire got up then, and went back inside the house, and put on a pot of water to boil the eggs for lunch.

Lady in Waiting

Barbara Johnson

There's something erotic," an ex-lover said to me
once, "about watching a woman put on her makeup."

It had been a long time since I'd thought of this
particular ex, but she came to mind as I prepared for
a night out with a new woman. Although this was
the first time Jana and I were going on a "date,"
we'd actually known each other for quite a few
months. When she finally suggested a night of dinner
and dancing, I was at first surprised and inclined to
say no. But then I'd looked at her as if seeing her

for the first time and wondered how I could not have thought of Jana as a potential lover.

She regarded me expectantly, her thin lips curved in that engaging grin that I'd noticed before but never registered. Her dark brown eyes were like melting chocolate, and all of a sudden they were melting me. She had a squarish face with a firm, strong chin and a nose that I'd always thought a bit too large but now seemed perfect. Her skin was an envious shade of golden brown, the kind for which rich socialites baked themselves for hours in tanning salons and on beaches. And her hair! What glorious hair — dark and thick and slightly wavy. And short, but not too short. I suddenly had an irresistible urge to run my fingers through it.

I saw her grin grow more hesitant as she waited for my answer, but I could say nothing. My eyes on their own accord followed the line of her throat to the broad shoulders dressed in blue flannel, followed the sweeping curves of her full breasts to her tapered waist, and then followed the rounded curves of her hips to the long legs encased in faded denim. The black cowboy boots with their two-inch heels made her slightly taller than me, just enough so that I had to look up at her. I suddenly caught her grin fading like the moon at dawn.

"Of course I'll go out with you," I said quickly, and was rewarded with a smile that dazzled me like no other. I felt myself blushing at the rush of feelings that overcame me.

"Great! I'll pick you up at seven. Put on your dancin' shoes, 'cause we're gonna be going all night."

And now the night was here. I knew Jana would

take me someplace elegant and special for dinner. Her reputation as a courtly butch was well known. I imagined that we'd go to one of the gay nightclubs for dancing rather than to some smoky bar. It had been a long time since I'd dressed up to go out. Jeans and a T-shirt would not do this time.

I decided to start the evening by spoiling myself with a warm, candlelit bath, scented with my favorite perfume. A few drops in the water were enough to infuse my skin with a lingering fragrance that would last all night long. I lay back in the steaming water and let my eyes close. Jana came to my mind. I wondered how she'd look tonight. How she'd appreciate how I looked.

I remembered the anticipation as I'd gone out and bought new clothes just for the occasion — a sexy silk dress of pale lavender with a deep V neckline and bell sleeves. The hem brushed an inch or two above my knees — not too short, but deliciously enticing. I'd found satin underwear, smooth, not lacy, so as not to mar the lines of the dress, and I'd bought the sheerest pantyhose that I could find. I wanted my legs to appear bare, but when Jana touched me, as I knew she would, she'd feel the sexy smoothness of the nylon. I'd found low-heeled satin shoes in the same shade as the dress. They shimmered in the light with every step I took, although I didn't intend for Jana to spend the evening looking at my feet.

I opened my eyes. Shadows from the candle flickered flirtatiously against the wall. The soft music of Tchaikovsky's "Sleeping Beauty" drifted in from the bedroom. I lathered up my sponge with a creamy soap. It felt sensual against my skin. I next shampooed my hair and put more drops of perfume into the rinse water. It was Opium, a scent that I knew Jana liked. I stepped out of the tub and wrapped myself in a thick pink towel fresh from the wash.

I came out of the bathroom and looked at my alarm clock. I had an hour before Jana would arrive. The anticipation gave me butterflies in my stomach. I sat on the bed and massaged my favorite after-bath oil into my still-damp skin, imagining Jana's hands rubbing the oil over my body. They'd be firm, yet gentle. As my hands brushed my breasts, I imagined her mouth taking in my nipples. I could feel my fingers running through her hair. I knew it would feel coarse and soft at the same time. With a deep sigh, I realized that if I didn't stop my fantasizing, I wouldn't be ready when Jana arrived. At least, not for dinner and dancing.

I looked in the full-length mirror. In the dim light, my skin glowed from the bath. The oil had given it an iridescent sheen. I wished that Jana were here now to see me. I felt desirable, something that I'd not felt in quite a while. I hadn't really been looking for a lover. That was why I'd never thought of Jana that way. She'd been a good friend, and we had fun together. For a brief moment I was afraid I'd made a terrible mistake in agreeing to go out with her. What if our friendship couldn't survive a transition to relationship? Suddenly panicky, I picked up the phone. I still had time to call her and cancel.

"Hello?"

The husky voice startled me. I couldn't believe I'd actually called.

"Uh, hi, Jana. It's me."

I could hear the smile in her voice. "Hey, sweetie.
I was just thinking about you. What's up?"

"Oh, nothing. I just wanted to hear your voice."

She laughed. The sound sent shivers up my spine.
"I'll be seeing you in a bit."

I looked at the clock. Oh God! Only 45 minutes
left. "Yes. See you then."

I hung up quickly. My new underwear was still in
its tissue paper. The ivory satin glided easily up my
legs. The panties were bikini, slung low on my hips.
The front-clasp bra was soft, yet held my breasts
firmly. No underwires this time. I looked in the
mirror again. I was curvy in all the right places. My
skin was smooth and pale. I frowned. Would Jana
think me washed out? Maybe I should have hit the
tanning salons? My light brown hair, still damp,
curled gently at my shoulders. I'd always liked its
texture and thickness, but thought the color kind of
drab. Maybe blonde highlights? Red? Well, now was
not the time to think about it. Left to air dry, my
hair would be a mass of unruly curls, but I quickly
blew it dry fairly straight. I looked in the mirror
again. My hair shone like polished wood. Highlights
didn't seem so necessary now.

I began pulling the expensive pantyhose gently up
my legs. I had to be extra careful so as not to snag
them. I had thought about buying real stockings, the
kind you need a garter belt for, but I knew the belt
would make a lumpy line around my waist. Still, the
pantyhose were completely sheer. I ran my hands
along my legs, smoothing out minuscule wrinkles.
Again, Jana came to mind as I mentally replaced my
hands with hers. She would be a little rough because

I was sure she hadn't much experience with such a delicate item of clothing. At least not with putting them on. The thought of snags suddenly didn't seem so bad.

With a concentrated effort, I banished Jana momentarily from my mind. I put on an ivory slip that matched my bra and panties and then slid the silk dress over my head. It flowed down over my body, draping just right. The sensual feel of it made goosebumps rise on my bare arms. I shivered.

I selected my jewelry carefully. The Y necklace with its amethyst pendant twinkled invitingly in the deep V of my dress. I brushed my hair behind my ears so the light caught the blaze of matching amethyst in my earlobes. I decided against a watch or bracelet, but added a simple silver ring.

My final step — putting on my makeup. That's when I'd thought of my ex. She used to sit on the toilet and watch me. In the beginning, it made me nervous, but then I got so used to it that I missed it terribly when we broke up. The memory made me smile, and I wondered how she was doing now.

I applied the makeup with a light touch. A little foundation, a brush of powder and blush, pearly shadow on my eyelids, and lots of mascara. I used violet — it brought out the blue of my eyes. I decided against a bold lipstick, choosing instead one with a faint lavender tint. A bit of cherry-flavored gloss made my lips shiny and, in my opinion, very kissable. I dabbed more Opium behind my ears, along my collarbone, between my breasts, behind my knees, and on my wrists and ankles — special places where a woman's mouth could drive me wild. Not just any woman's, but Jana's.

I glanced once more at the clock. She would be here in ten minutes. I slipped on my new shoes and descended the stairs to the living room. I turned the lights down low and put on romantic music. Then I sat on my comfortable couch to wait for my date.

The Saxophone Player
Lee Lynch

Three weeks to the day after Mandy Tolliver arrived in Chicago, she slept with the piano player. A saxophonist, she hadn't much use for ragtime in her own repertoire, but Ruby earned enough at a supper club as a sultry long-haired torch singer to support a passion for the music. Ruby composed her rags at the lavender piano downstairs in the collective where both she and Mandy lived. Mandy spent a lot of time in those first weeks next to the piano, trying to find a way to accompany Ruby on sax.

To tell the truth, Mandy thought now, stretched above Ruby, pubic bone to fleshy mound, as they made their own rhythm, the torch singer Ruby turned her on as much as Ruby the composer. It was crooning Ruby she followed on the sax in her head, as she felt herself clench and unclench inside, riding the quickening hips of this self-styled Lauren Bacall beneath her. Ruby was singing her way into orgasm.

The Gilded Carriage had been lit outside with a gold neon sign. A cocktail glass was tilted off the final "e." Bubbles winked in the glass as if rising into the dark Chicago night.

Inside, the maitre d' looked Mandy and her friend Lorna up and down, but seated them fairly close to the piano when Mandy tipped him. Her heart raced to see Ruby approach the piano in that form-molding yellow dress. Ruby made playing look easier than melting butter, and the notes she sang wafted above the clinking dinnerware like weightless precious jewels.

After Ruby had come her flesh felt like melting butter too, it was so warm, so softened. Mandy rose to her elbows and looked down at the satisfied green eyes, the tangled, honey-streaked hair.

"Musicians and good dancers," said Ruby softly into Mandy's ear. "Poets, too."

"We have something in common?"

"Rhythm," Ruby said. "We have a way of communicating through rhythm, don't you think?" Her voice was husky from smoke-filled clubs.

Mandy rolled her long, androgynous body aside. "How you ended up in this dyke collective I'll never know," she said. "You're something else."

"It's simple, Butchie." They'd done a lot of music together, but not much talking. "Men have their place in the world, but it's not in my bed or in my head. The money they pay me to look like they wish their wives did just about shelters me here, feeds me and buys me the fancy clothes I need. Plus, I believe in alternative living spaces, so women like me —" she turned to Mandy and prodded her between small breasts with a fingernail painted pink, "and you have some choices."

Mandy loved being called Butchie.

The first time had been after Ruby's last set, when Mandy and Lorna had met her at the back door to the Gilded Carriage. Mandy wished she'd brought her sax — to serenade Ruby when she appeared after her last set.

They took the elevated home so they could see the Christmas lights, and rocked north through the city high, smiley, full of a warm energy Mandy was tempted to call love. Love of her new life, her new friends, her soon-to-be-new lover?

Every time she looked at Ruby in that fake fur, yellow dress flashing underneath, stockinged ivory legs smooth and seductively crossed, she wanted her. And knew she looked good herself tonight, slim and erect in the black performing suit, ruffled pink shirt open at the neck to show a fine gold chain.

"Hi there, Butchie," Ruby had said inside the door to her room, punctuating their first kiss with a low whistle.

"How about you, Butchie?" Ruby asked, rising, pushing Mandy back and leaning over her. Both her hair and her pear-sized breasts grazed Mandy.

God, she thought, growing short of breath, at least wet down there. But it was hard enough getting naked for a woman, never mind lying back and letting go. Sometimes it seemed as if she wasn't pursuing women at all, but the elusive orgasm, and that if she ever found the woman who could release her she'd never, never, never leave.

Ruby went on. "Do you come by the rhythm method too?" Long, strong fingers massaged her genitals, firm and gentle fingers, daring and frightening. "No? Then let's try a different tune."

The loose hair left a trail of sensation down her body, made a tent of itself that screened out Ruby's mouth, her tongue. All Mandy could see were two beautiful hands spread across her pelvis to either side of Ruby's hair. She lay her fingers between Ruby's, set up a tattoo, which Ruby joined. She watched the fingers jump and touch, like accompaniment to her anxious, craving heart. Over and over, she pictured Ruby in the yellow dress while she strained with her

thigh muscles. But no magic happened. She might as
well go back to being stone butch for all she got out
of taking her pants off.

Ruby lifted her head, hair streaming, face wet like
someone rising from the sea. She narrowed her eyes
as Mandy propped herself on her arms. "Is anything
happening for you, Butchie?"

Mandy tried to shrug, but her position kept her
gestureless, her mind, wordless. "Sometimes —" She
longed for her saxophone. A blues number about
yearning and denial, about loving and walking away
when all you wanted was to stay — "Sometimes I
don't connect very well."

"With me? Is there something else I should be
doing?"

As if those pink-polished fingers against Mandy's
jutting hip bones could do wrong. She pulled Ruby
up, held onto her. "No. What's wrong is inside me."

Now. Now was the time to rise and dress, to act
cool, like it didn't matter, to take the sax and find a
road job. Two, three weeks, a month out and she
could try someone new. The yellow dress, the pears
flat against her sweat-moist chest — all would become
the stuff of fantasy. She squeezed her eyes shut to
keep the tears inside, but only succeeded in squeezing
them out. "Ruby," she said hoarsely, "You're very
special. I wish —" *I could play you my blues.*

Everyone in the collective had stayed home, bringing lovers, exes, friends, even family. Mandy was
nervous: she wasn't sure they'd like "Rag With Saxo-

phone." Nor was she certain she wanted publicly to play the blues Ruby had written, "Mandy's Move." But if they couldn't be lovers — and Mandy hadn't been willing to work things through at the pace Ruby needed — they could at least play together.

She wore a red shirt, open low, and pink suspenders with black velour pants. Ruby, at the piano, was in soft gray, in her hair the orange flower Mandy had presented with a lover's flourish. Lorna had rigged spotlights in the big living room. At her signal someone switched off the overheads. Ruby played softly as the chandelier, on a dimmer, came up. There was no one in the room now but the two musicians and their instruments.

They played some lively numbers, a love song or two, and the audience was warm but subdued, as if giving them their reins. Ruby was fun to play with, tricky, a challenge. Then it was time for "Mandy's Move."

It started as a rolling, honky-tonk blues, but when Ruby dropped back and Mandy wailed in on her tenor sax, she could feel the shiver in the room. She swayed as she blew, played Ruby's rhythm, played her own sad hopes too, exactly the way Ruby wrote them.

When the sweat began to make even her fingers slick, she turned to smiling Ruby and dipped the saxophone. Ruby nodded and came back in. No one could sustain such heart-rending stuff alone.

Girl Talk

Julia Watts

I know, I know. I'm your friend from work, and we can't sleep in the same bed," I recited for the tenth time. "God, Judy, for such a big, bad butch, you sure are a closet case."

"Stop calling me that. Am I a closet case even though I'm out to everybody in the universe except my mom?"

"No comment." We were driving through the depths of south Alabama, with nothing in sight but endless scrub pines and the occasional barbecue stand. The Melissa Etheridge song on the tape player was our only reminder that we were still on a planet where people like us existed.

"Di, you just don't know what it's like being the child of old parents. It changes things — it's like dealing with two generation gaps instead of one."

Judy had been what old Southern women call a "change-of-life baby" — and an only child to boot. Her mother had named her after her favorite film star, Judy Garland, in hopes that her daughter would grow up to be as glamorous as her namesake. I think it was Judy's name that first drew me to her. A big butch dyke named after a gay male icon was deliciously unexpected.

Judy and I had been dating for six months, and as far as I was concerned, she was the woman I had been waiting for ever since the moment I caught my first glimpse of Diana Rigg on *The Avengers* and realized I wasn't like all the other little girls.

Judy, however, wasn't as quick to commit. I had been pestering her to move in with me for the past three months, and she kept hemming and hawing about how she wasn't sure her dog and my cat would get along and what a pain it is to divide up household chores.

Recently, I had backed off on the issue, figuring that dating Judy happily ever after was better than no future with her at all. And then, like a bolt out of the lavender, she invited me to go with her to visit her mother, on the condition that my true identity would not be revealed. Still the invitation could be interpreted as a sign of commitment . . . kinda, sorta.

I had heard dozens of entertaining stories about

Judy's mother — about her days as a debutante in Birmingham, about the time during the war when she slashed a soldier's face with a broken beer bottle because he had made a lewd comment to her, about the four husbands she had married and buried: the first two for love, the last two for money. I was excited about meeting her, but also a little terrified.

Reading my mind, Judy said, "Don't be nervous about dealing with her, hon. When in doubt, just compliment her on her appearance. She won't give a damn whether you like her cooking or think the house looks nice, but if you tell her how thin she is or what a nice manicure she has, she'll be your friend for life."

I surveyed Judy's stout, muscular body and gnawed-to-the-nubs fingernails. "How did a woman like her end up with you for a daughter?"

Judy shrugged. "Never say that God lacks a sense of humor."

The house was a large red brick rancher with a porch lined with rocking chairs. It was the kind of house that wouldn't draw much notice in a city but was palatial by the standards of a small, south Alabama town. Judy led me to the back door, explaining, "Mama always insists that family and friends use the back door. That way, if the front doorbell rings, she knows it's somebody who's trying to sell her something or give her a *Watchtower.*"

The back door swung open before we had a chance to knock. Standing before us was a striking, elderly woman with white washed-and-set-at-the-beauty-shop hair, Lauren Bacall cheekbones and Joan Crawford shoulders. Her long nails were painted shell pink, and the ring finger of each hand glittered with an obscenely huge diamond. She gave Judy a once-over, then said, with an accent that masked malice with magnolias, "Well, look at you. You're sure not gettin' any thinner, are you?"

Judy didn't miss a beat, which gave me the impression that what I had just heard was a traditional greeting. "Mama, this is Diane, a friend of mine from work."

"It's a pleasure to meet you, Mrs. . . . Mrs. . . . ." I stalled. Judy's last name was Wyler, but her mom had had two husbands since Judy's dad. How could I have forgotten to ask Judy her mom's current last name?

"Just call me Theda, honey." She smiled, a little moue. "I've had so many last names I barely remember 'em myself." She patted Judy on the shoulder. "You girls come on in." Before I could even orient myself to my new environment, Theda announced, "Well, I guess we'd better go ahead and eat. The Braves game starts at eight."

I was confused. The kitchen, which was decorated in the dark browns and avocado greens of the '70s, showed no signs that any cooking had been done there in recent history. Despite the cavelike quality the color scheme bestowed on it, the kitchen was spotless in the way that only a non-cook's kitchen can be.

My questions were answered when Theda began rifling through the freezer. She produced three packages of Lean Cuisine frozen dinners and declared, "All right, I've got spaghetti with meat sauce, vegetable lasagna and macaroni and cheese. Who wants what?"

I got stuck with the macaroni and cheese. We sat at the kitchen table, each with a little box of microwaved food, a can of Diet Coke and a plastic fork. I was amazed. Before I took Judy home the first time, my mom called me on three different occasions for the sole purpose of discussing possible menus. I glanced nervously at the bottle of ketchup and jar of pickles which sat in the center of the table, fearful that I would be considered rude if I didn't find some use for them.

"So, Diane, you must eat a lot of these low-calorie dinners," Theda said. "You've got a cute little figure on you." She pronounced figure "figga."

"Uh . . . thanks," I said, uncomfortable with the idea that my lover's mom was scoping out my bod.

"If there's anything a man likes, it's a cute figure," Theda went on. "Put on some stockings and heels, smile and cross your legs real pretty, and a man'll do anything you want."

"Mama!" Judy protested.

"Judy always thinks I shock people. I'm not shockin' you, am I, Diane?"

"No, ma'am."

"Well, I figure it's just us girls together. What can we talk about if not men?"

What indeed? I stared down at my food, confident that if I caught Judy's eye, I'd have a giggling fit the likes of which I hadn't had since I was twelve years old and forced to sit quietly in church.

"I always tell Judy she could do better in the

looks department," Theda was saying. "She may have got her daddy's stoutness, but she's still got my eyes and mouth, don't you think, Diane?"

"Um . . . yeah." I shifted uncomfortably. Given my rather intimate knowledge of Judy's mouth, I certainly didn't want to think of it as belonging to her mother.

"Yes, she could turn some heads, all right," Theda said, staring at her daughter's face. "Put on a dress every once in a while, let those awful fingernails grow out —"

"Mama, I fix computers for a living. I can't have long nails that are gonna get stuck in the machinery."

"She's such a tomboy, Diane. Always been more interested in fixin' things than in fixin' herself up. When she was little, I wanted her to take dance lessons, to be like Judy Garland — that's who I named her after, you know." She pushed her half-eaten spaghetti away. "But all she wanted to do was follow her daddy around and help him build things. Birdhouses, bookshelves, kitchen cabinets — you name it, they built it."

"I think it's great that Judy's so . . ." I searched for a word. "Handy."

"Oh, it's wonderful for a woman to know how to do things for herself," Theda said. "Of course, that's no reason for her to let her looks go. And sometimes, when you're around a man, it's good to let on you don't know quite as much as you do."

"It's not nineteen-fifty anymore, Mama. Women don't have to play dumb to get what they want."

"Oh, don't they?" Theda paused to admire the

diamonds on her fingers. "Well, we've been havin' this argument since you were sixteen years old. You get your power your way, I'll get mine my way." She turned to me. "Now, Diane, what you need is some color on your lips and eyes, and you've *got* to do somethin' about those eyebrows."

In terms of bushiness, my eyebrows do lie somewhere between Brooke Shields' and Brezhnev's. But I've always had a very minimalist beauty philosophy: Don't mess with what's already there; just make sure your teeth are clean and you don't smell bad, and you're good to go.

Even though I hate baseball, I was relieved when the Braves game started. Theda and Judy were riveted to the screen, Judy gnawing her nails and Theda smoking cigarette after cigarette with Bette Davis aplomb.

Judy and I live in Atlanta. She took me to a Braves game once in the early days of our relationship. She was so transfixed by the action on the field she appeared incapable of conversation, so to relieve my boredom, I kept downing little plastic cups of beer. By the end of the ninth inning, I was so drunk I fell down the steps as we were leaving our seats. When my coworkers inquired about the Ace bandage on my ankle the next day, I proudly told them it was a baseball injury.

After the game was over, Theda stood up, stretched demurely and announced that it was her bedtime, with the implication that it should be ours, too.

After she was safely out of the room, Judy whispered, "She's a piece of work, isn't she?"

"I'll say." I looked around to make sure we had

some privacy. "Hon, why were there pickles and ketchup on the dinner table?" Those nonsequitur condiments had been bothering me all night.

"You don't think we're trash, do you?"

Apparently, this was supposed to answer my question. Since inappropriate condiments seemed to be a sensitive issue, I decided not pursue it.

Judy stood and stretched. "Well, time for bed."

"Really?" It was an hour and a half before our usual bedtime. "Yep." She walked right past me.

"Judy!" I barked, then lowered my voice, "Don't I get a kiss?"

She blew me a kiss from several feet away and then padded on down the hall. Thank God this was just a weekend visit. If I had to spend a week at Judy's mother's, I'd die from lack of affection.

I woke up the next morning thoroughly disoriented. I saw the *Reader's Digest* Condensed Novels on the nightstand and the needlepointed poem titled "A Prayer for Friends of the Aged" on the wall and wondered briefly if I was really an old woman who had just awakened from a strange dream in which she was a twenty-nine-year-old lesbian.

Then I felt her eyes on me.

Theda was sitting in the corner, perfectly coiffed and made up, smoking and staring at me. How long had she been watching me sleep? Where was Judy? And what was the name of that horror movie where the crazy woman played by Tallulah Bankhead tries to torture her daughter-in-law to death? "Uh . . . good morning."

"It's not mornin' now. I've never seen a person sleep so sound."

"Where's Judy?" I tried to sound calm, but my voice cracked.

"She went to lunch with her cousin Cindy over at the Western Sizzlin. I told her to go on without you. That way, you and I can have some time for girl talk."

No doubt about it, as soon as Judy got back, I was going to kill her. I could already see the headlines: *Sapphic Slaying in South Alabama.* "Girl talk . . . great," I said feebly.

"You wouldn't like Cindy anyway. She's a religious nut. I bet she's already loaded down poor Judy with all those damn pamphlets she carries." She stubbed out her cigarette. "Get on up. I made you some coffee."

Theda's coffee could best be described as chunky style.

"Can I fix you some breakfast?" she offered.

Remembering the Lean Cuisine from the night before, I was apprehensive about what she might pull out of the freezer. "No, thanks." I spied a fruit bowl on the counter. "I'll just snag one of these apples."

"Are you sure? I've got some of them Breakfast Burritos."

"I'm sure." I was, too.

"That's how you keep that cute little figure — you eat like a bird. You know, all mornin' I've been thinkin' about somethin' fun we can do while Judy's away. I'll tell you what. Why don't you go ahead and take your shower, and then meet me back in my bedroom. Don't bother gettin' dressed. I've got a robe you can wear."

"Uh . . . What are we going to do?"

"It's a surprise!" She clapped her hands with little-girl delight. "I think I'm gonna put on some music. Is Englebert Humperdinck all right?"

"Sure." Were we dealing with a "like mother, like daughter" situation here? Was Theda planning to seduce me to the strains of "Red Sails in the Sunset"? Just what the hell was going on here?

Too curious to do otherwise, I entered Theda's room, dressed only in my underwear and her robe. She was sitting on the edge of the bed. "Let's go in the bathroom," she said inexplicably.

"Okay." Her powder blue bathroom was a shrine to femininity, with lighted mirrors and jars full of cotton balls and makeup sponges and bottle after bottle of nail polish.

"Sit down on the commode," she ordered.

Dumbly, I did as I was told.

She hovered over me. "Do you know what I'm gonna do to you, darlin'?"

"I have absolutely no idea."

She took my face in her hands and looked at me intently. "I'm gonna give you . . . a makeover."

"A what?"

"Oh, I saw it on a talk show the other day." She was rifling through a drawer that overflowed with cosmetics. "This is gonna be so much fun . . . Ah, here they are." She held up a gleaming pair of tweezers. "First, we gotta do somethin' about those eyebrows."

She leaned over me and yanked a clump of hair from my brow. "Ow!" I yelled, kicking her involuntarily.

"Oh, it's not that bad," she said. "After you've

plucked 'em a few dozen times, you lose all the feelin' there. Of course, if it hurts too much, we could just shave 'em off and paint some on."

Yeah, that would be great, I thought. That way, I could paint on eyebrows to match my mood . . . two raised eyebrows on days when I wanted to look surprised, one raised eyebrow when I wanted to look incredulous. "I don't think so," I said.

"All right, then. Pluckin' it is." She ripped out another clump.

"Yow!"

"Hang on just a minute. I'll bring you somethin' that'll make it better."

She returned with a tumbler of amber liquid. "Here, drink this sherry. It'll still hurt, but you won't mind as much."

"I don't know. It's awfully early."

"Oh, go ahead. It's not every day a girl gets a free makeover."

I drank as instructed. Something about this woman made me helpless in her presence. Now I knew how her four husbands had felt.

"There, now," she said. "That's not so bad, is it?"

"No, not really — ow!" I took a fortifying sip, like a cowboy swilling whiskey while his buddy removed a bullet from his leg.

"Now, let's see . . . You've got good skin. You just need a dab of foundation. You don't wanna overdo it. You want men to think you're a lady, but that you might not be a lady all the time, if you know what I mean."

Silently I cursed Judy for running off with her

Bible-banging cousin and leaving me trapped in the Land of Compulsory Heterosexuality. I gulped down some more sherry.

"A little kohl around the eyes, I think. You've got smoky eyes."

In the past, when women have complimented my eyes, it's not been when they were applying makeup to them.

"And a little color there. Now kind of smack your lips together . . . that's good. So what is it you do at the company where Judy works?"

"I'm sort of a glorified secretary, really."

"Nothin' wrong with that. Everybody knows it's secretaries that run businesses. The big boss men get all the money, and the secretaries do all the work."

"I agree. Except my boss is a woman."

"Well, how 'bout that! And you met Judy at work?" She was brushing something onto my cheeks.

"Yeah, when she started doing some consulting work for our company."

"And how long have y'all been datin'?"

"Six months." I answered automatically, then realized what she had asked and what I had said.

She laughed. "Well, those cheeks don't need any more blush now!"

"You . . . know?"

"Honey, I've known since Judy was practically a toddler. Why, she's always been the butchiest little thing that ever come down the pike!" She turned her attentions to my hair, attacking it with a curling iron. "You're the first girlfriend she's had the nerve to bring home, so I consider that a good sign . . . for me and you both."

The fact that my mouth was hanging open made it difficult to speak. "So why don't you just tell her?"

"Honey, it's not my job to tell her. It's her job to tell me."

"So all that talk about men and her putting on a dress —"

"I'm just hopin' that someday I'll make her mad enough that she'll just come right out and tell me."

I laughed. "Judy's right. You are a piece of work!"

"Oh, I know I am! I don't know why that daughter of mine thinks I'm too dull-witted to know what a lesbian is. When I was livin' in Birmingham durin' the war, I worked in a factory *full* of dykes." She looked at herself admiringly in the mirror. "And let me tell you, honey. Those butches *loved* me."

When Theda was through with me, I looked like a '40s movie star. My usually lank hair fell in a soft wave over the right side of my face. My eyes, which *are* smoky, though I had never noticed it before, were made up just enough to make me look slightly exotic. My lips and nails were ruby red, and my eyebrows . . . well, they'd grow back.

Still, I was glamorous. I wore a simple black dress and nylons Theda loaned me, but I had to walk around in stocking feet because my feet were two sizes larger than hers. It was just as well; I can't walk in heels anyway. When I looked in Theda's full-length mirror, the woman who looked back at me was the woman in my fantasies — not the woman I fantasize about having, but the woman I fantasize about being when Judy makes love to me. I had become the femme of my fantasies: sexy, smart, strong in her femininity.

"Theda, can I have one of your cigarettes? I don't want to smoke it, just hold it." I held the cigarette, struck a vampish pose in front of the mirror, then dissolved into a fit of giggles.

Theda slapped me playfully on the butt. "I was hopin' I'd convince you to do yourself up like this every day, and here you are, thinkin' it's Halloween." I heard the back door open. "Well, Diana, it sounds like your 'friend from work' is home." She disappeared down the hall calling, "Well, there you are! You were gone so long we thought Cindy had converted you."

I walked down the hall into the den. When Judy saw me, her eyes softened like they did during our most private moments, then she caught herself, and looked down at her tennis shoes.

"Doesn't she look pretty, Judy?" Theda said. "Why, if you got yourself up like that once in a while, you could find a boyfriend in no time." She slapped her daughter on her back. "I'm gonna go outside and check the mail, girls, and then I think I just might sit out on the porch and smoke me a cigarette."

I should have been surprised at how obvious she was being about giving us a few minutes alone, but by this point, Theda wouldn't have surprised me if she had appeared wearing a leather bustier and wielding a whip.

I sat down on the couch and looked up at Judy. "So how do you like your mother's artwork?"

"It's, uh . . . You're, uh . . . Do you think you could dress up like that for me at home sometime?"

I crossed my legs in a way that would've made

Theda proud. "Your place or mine?" The femme in
me was bold, just like in my fantasies.

"Actually, uh . . ." Judy sat down next to me and
took my hand. "I've been thinking, what with my
lease running out and all . . . maybe we should look
for a place together."

I fluttered my eyelashes and put on my best
Southern belle accent. "Why, Ms. Wyler, if ah didn't
know better, ah'd say you wuh proposin' to me!"

"Actually, I was thinking of us living in sin."

I smiled. "It's the only way to live." I grabbed
her by the collar. "C'mere."

"Uh . . . do you think it's safe?"

"Do you care?"

We kissed, her hands stroking my soft waves of
hair, my red-painted fingernails scratching her back.
When we pulled apart, we were both out of breath.

"You've got lipstick on your face."

She took a tissue from her pocket and began
frantically scrubbing. "Is it gone?"

"Mm-hmm."

"God, I can't believe I kissed you like that here,
but you just look so . . ." She erupted into nervous
laughter. "There's probably some deeply Freudian
symbolism in this situation; I just thank God I'm not
smart enough to see it." She lowered her voice to a
whisper. "You know, sometimes I get so tired of tippy-
toeing around my personal life when I'm talking to
Mama. It gets old, being vague, avoiding pronouns.
Diane, what do you think she'd say if I told her
about us?"

"You might be surprised, Judy." I laid my head on
her shoulder. "You might be surprised."

Fair Weather
Janet E. McClellan

Two days before Free Night at the Kansas State Fair found Jessie Cameron trying to fix a flat tire on her late-model truck. Her calloused hands gripped the tire iron as she moved her strong back and arms into position. She shifted her weight and pushed, using her well-muscled legs in the gritting effort. The extra weight of the camper seemed to make the truck hunker down to the road. Jessie cursed. She was supposed to have been in Hutchinson, Kansas, two days ago to help set up the rigging, adjust the cables and check the maintenance on the giant Ferris wheel. Her luck seemed to abandon her just when she desperately needed to keep the work she'd found. Her once-reliable transportation was threatening to get her fired. The flat tire was the latest in a long list of grievances against the old truck and the way her life seemed to go.

"That's what I get," she mumbled to herself while she tried to twist a lug nut off. "Last time I let some station attendant use a hydraulic on my tires." Her exertions caused sweat to stream out of her dark short hair, down her forehead, and drip stingingly into her eyes. She cursed the mechanic as the plains wind blew the grit and September pollens around her face.

Three hours later she and the truck limped onto the fairgrounds with the tire precariously fastened on by the three lug nuts she'd managed not to strip. Worn, weary and hungry, she ignored her protesting stomach and parked beside the RV belonging to the manager of the rides. She knocked on the door and walked in.

"What?" a gruff voice called through the dark smoky interior.

Jessie coughed in the rank thick cigar smoke. "I'm Cameron. Here to check and run the big Ferris wheel," Jessie said, trying not to breathe. As the smoke streamed past her out into the fresh air, she wished she could follow it.

"Where the hell have you been? Christ, you look like shit. Been tying one on? If that thing's not working, it'll cost us a piece of the contract and your ass," he ranted.

"I'm here now. You gonna tell me where it's at or jack your jaw some more?" Jessie asked assertively. If she squinted, she could barely make out a large soft shape, ham-sized hands and a balding head floating behind his desk.

"Whatever. Get over there past the main pavilion and do me some good. Near the horse stables. Past the end of that row of wooden buildings. Got a green roof. Can't miss it. A crew been unloading the thing while I wondered if you'd show," he said, wheezing.

"I need an advance. Two hundred for the maintenance. I'm to get five for the week," Jessie announced.

"You got to be kidding?"

"No. I'm flat busted broke. I'll take a hundred and you can owe me the six. That's in my contract. I imagine you got a copy?"

"Don't push it, Cameron," the man said as he drew a small blue battered cash box out of a drawer. "Here. You gotta live on this till Sunday. I didn't take you on to raise," he said and tossed the bills across the desk. Jessie walked slowly to the desk, picked up the money and retreated into the fresh air.

She drove across the grounds and found a team of riggers worrying the hundreds of parts of the Ferris wheel. She found the straw boss, a thin wiry little man who initially called her sir when he noticed how her six-foot frame towered over him. He grinned at her like he thought he was funny but corrected himself and apologized when she smiled menacingly at him through her straight white teeth.

Jessie pulled the workers away from their misguided chores and steered them toward the doing

of first things first. The tasks to which she redirected
them amounted to inventorying every part of the
huge ride. Every nut, bolt, stay, brace, cable, pulley,
cage and chair had to be accounted for before she
would let them begin the choreographed act of
assembling the beast. She was in her element. A
perfectionist and proud of it, she wanted a safe,
well-working monster ride for people to enjoy. She
would not tolerate the likelihood of potential mishaps,
threats of disaster, or the possi- bilities of another's
injury haunting her. While the crew checked the
parts, Jessie tuned the Ferris wheel's motor.

At ten that night Jessie was satisfied with the
motor and primary assemblage of the structure, and
exhausted. She let the crew go but not before admonishing them to be back at six in the morning.
She had less than twenty hours to get the thing
together and tested before the first customer climbed
on board.

As they left, Jessie stretched her aching shoulders,
packed her tools and drove down the central fairway
to her assigned parking place at the roustabout campground. Inside the camper she grabbed a clean pair
of jeans, shirt, underwear, soap and towels. She
wanted to get a shower, fix supper and have an ice-
cold beer. Not necessarily in that order. Jessie rolled
her stuff into a bundle, locked the camper door and
marched off toward the glow of halogen lights standing guard around the tiny cinderblock building that
housed the campground's showers. Jessie hoped the
hour was late enough that the others had finished
and gone back to their RVs or campers. She didn't

want to stand in line but prayed they'd left her a little hot water.

To her delight, the water was hot, plentiful and bursting with steamy force. She lathered, rinsed, lathered again and washed the knots of pain and ache from her body. Finished, she stood quietly under the rushing water and let it pound the top of her head, across her shoulders and down her back and legs in searing cascades. The wet meditation calmed and refreshed her.

Jessie walked out of the building and felt the warm night air ripple across her still-damp arms. She shook her hair and ran a hand through it. Sweeping it into place, she looked up and saw a star shoot across the night sky. A smile spread over her face at the lucky omen. Jessie knew she needed some good luck for a change and thought the new job might be a good start. She had some money and the promise of more at the end of the week. All she had to do was put up with throngs of farmers, ranchers, whatever Kansas had that passed for city folks, and their screaming kids for a few days.

Maybe, she thought, maybe she could hook up with the carnies for a few towns or even find work for a while in Hutchinson. That would be good, she mused, and wondered what it would be like to stay in one spot for a bit.

Suddenly, the sound of thunder detonated behind her. Jessie turned just in time to feel something enormous and deafening descending on her. A great form rushed toward her, veered at the last moment and assembled itself out of the swirling of tempests.

Shock mesmerized her and rooted her where she stood.

Dust, sand, dirt and fluttering bits of trash settled as Jessie watched a woman jerk determinedly against the straining reins of a horse. The woman's body, encased in a costume of tight royal blue laced in seamed white spangles, danced and clung to the four-legged cyclone. The satin textures of the clothes and the jaunty angle of her hat were wildly at odds with the defiant fury of the horse. The horse's eyes rolled back in its head, exposing stark white orbs. Its belligerent body strained against the rider's mastery of its frenzy.

"Nasty-tempered beast!" the woman yelled. She pulled the long leather straps back sharply to her chest. In mad protest the horse began to rear, topple and fall in a terrible swelling of disaster.

Time seemed to slow while Jessie watched the woman stand in the stirrups and swing her right leg out and away. For a moment horse and rider were suspended in a dark fatal dance. Then, as the horse fell, the rider stepped back from her last toehold in the left stirrup, sprang away and landed standing on the ground. Her mount tumbled to his side but she kept hold of the reins.

The horse crashed screaming down to the dirt, rocked violently on his side and scrambled to his knees. On his feet again he instantly stopped his struggles. His sides heaved, withers shuddered, as the hysteria in his eyes flickered out.

Holding the leather reins with both hands, the dismounted rider walked slowly toward the horse, whispering to him in soft soothing tones.

"You witless, mean-spirited stud. You could have killed me. And I think you were trying," she said, running a leather-gloved hand down his neck, across the abrasions he'd inflicted on himself and over the flank. Still talking to him in a gentle voice, she looked around and noticed Jessie staring at her. "Oh, honey," she said and moved toward Jessie, but the pull of the reins held her back. She looked confused, trying to figure out how to go to Jessie without alarming the horse. "Are you all right? I thought for sure he had you."

The dust and grime of the near collision had settled on and around Jessie. She could feel the fine grit clinging to her skin and hair. She realized she'd almost been trampled to death.

"Don't come near me." Jessie's voice boiled unevenly.

"Now, honey, I didn't mean —"

"Stop it with the honey thing," Jessie interrupted, and watched a flicker of a smile cross the woman's face.

"Are you okay?" the woman persisted and stepped toward Jessie.

"Stay back. I want you and that horse from hell at a safe distance," Jessie said, pointedly ordering the woman to stay put.

"Oh, now, old Roger Storm-Dodger here doesn't mean any harm. He just needs a firm hand occasionally. Keeps him in line." She rubbed the horse's nose lovingly. "Nothing wrong with a firm hand, is there?" She smiled that slow smile at Jessie again.

Jessie felt the woman's gaze move across her body, linger here and there, loiter a second or two as it danced back to her face. A startled thud hit Jessie in the solar plexus and warmed her from navel to knees as astonishment overtook her. Caution leaped through Jessie's mind and her eyes narrowed on the woman. She wondered if they always grew them green as grass in Kansas.

"I need a shower," Jessie said, figuring that the sweetheart of the rodeo had no idea what she was saying or just how far it might get her. She waved a weary arm at the woman and turned away. "Hang me for sure," she muttered and walked back toward the showers.

Jessie took her second shower of the evening and watched the screen in her mind play fantasies starring the sultry rodeo confection. Desire swept through her like a hot wind. Piqued at herself, she turned off the hot water and stood with chattering teeth under a violent cold spray. Naked and shivering, she dusted off her clothes while listening to the irate rumblings of her empty stomach. When she emerged from the building the second time, she poked her head out of the door. It was safe. No wide, wild horses or reckless women could be seen or heard in any direction. Whistling a little sadly to herself, Jessie started to walk back toward her truck and the safety of the camper.

"Wait up." A woman's dusky alto reached Jessie's ears.

Jessie turned and watched the woman jog toward her on the high heels of royal blue boots. The cool relief of the shower vanished. She watched the curve of the woman's legs, the smooth clinging fabric, and the sleek muscles as they bunched and relaxed again.

A head taller, Jessie knew how well she would fit into her arms.

"Way over my head. Somebody's daddy will shoot me for sure," Jessie grumbled a warning to herself. "Course, they'd have to get me in their sights first," she added mockingly. "What do you want?" Jessie asked when the woman stopped and stood close beside her.

"Be civil, now. I . . . I was wondering if . . . if you'd had anything to eat yet?" she asked through her electric smile.

"No," Jessie answered slowly. "Not in quite some time." She took hold of the woman's arm. "What did you have in mind?" She gauged the woman to be not much younger than she was and way over the legal limit. A keeper.

"What's your name?" the woman asked, and fell into stride beside Jessie.

"Jessie Cameron. And you are?"

"Camille Becker. I figured the least I could do is take you to dinner. There is a hot spot or two in town," she said, looking up into Jessie's eyes.

"I shouldn't doubt it," Jessie said, almost choking. "But I already set a couple of small steaks out for my grill. So, maybe you'd join me? That is, unless someone is expecting you elsewhere?" Jessie wondered what sort of trouble she was walking into.

"No one that counts, and I'd be delighted to have supper with you."

The camper had always felt roomy to Jessie. With Camille inside, it became close, cramped and difficult to navigate in. She couldn't move without bumping or brushing against Camille. Every time she turned,

Camille was there, soft, smiling and waiting. Camille's touchy opportunism made Jessie's desire oscillate with uncharacteristic timidity. Willing control, Jessie seasoned the steaks with care while her head spun cautionary tales about big city dykes and farmers' daughters.

"You're kinda shy for a big girl," Camille said, suddenly leaning her body against Jessie's back and running her hands along the muscle defined in Jessie's arms.

"Do you know what you are doing, cowgirl?"

"Yes, but do you know what you're doing?" Camille moved her hands to play across Jessie's ribs and breasts and stroke down to her stomach.

"I will in just a second." Jessie breathed in deeply, turned and pulled Camille to her. Camille clung to her and Jessie smelled the scent of light roses from Camille's thick blond hair. Camille kissed the trembling heartbeat in Jessie's throat. Jessie swept her hands down Camille's silky shirt and up again to cup and mold her breasts. She touched the buttoned seams and found snaps instead.

Goddess, will wonders never cease, snap-off shirts! Jessie beamed and pulled at the material until it magically opened. Camille swooned lightly when Jessie freed her breasts from their cotton-crossed restraints. She buried her face in the sweet heat and flicked her tongue across taut nipples. She breathed in hot hunger, reached around, lifted and carried Camille to the cab-over bed. With smooth purposeful motions Jessie laid Camille on the bedspread, nudged out the light switch with her elbow and followed Camille up into the low space.

Clothes and elbows, knees and belt buckles, fervor and swollen need battled briefly under the low ceiling until flesh touched flesh. Jessie's hands touched silk and skin, scoring it with anxious, work-roughened fingers. Caresses learned impatience as Jessie's control was tortured by Camille's beguiling tongue that coursed wickedly in her mouth. Tingling chain-reactions pleasured their sweet labors of love.

Jessie crouched above Camille and slowly moved a knee to touch the mound and soft hair between Camille's legs. Camille moved against her, arching, spreading wide to offer herself as Jessie steadied her arm and lifted Camille against her. She could feel shudders running through Camille and pressed her advantage. Her face hung suspended over Camille's while her body rocked and teased the kindled fire searing through Camille. She lowered her mouth and let her tongue devour Camille's breasts, sucking in delirious strokes while deftly nibbling at the full tender flesh and provoking quivering sighs. Jessie sought her mouth again, and Camille's lips trembled.

Slowly she rolled over, gently urging to Camille to follow. She slipped her hand down, let it brush between Camille's thighs until she began to move against her fingers. Their sweaty tempo leaped to elation and the mingling of coincidental sighs.

"I . . . want . . ." Camille's staccato voice pleaded as Jessie kneaded her in wet ardent urging.

"You do," Jessie whispered. "You do want so beautifully."

Camille arched her back, brushing the camper's ceiling, as Jessie's fingers sought the molten hollow inside her. She gaped open, bucked and plunged down, her beseeching delirium triggered by Jessie's hand. Camille vaulted and quivered to Jessie's whispered, melodic encouragements. Then Jessie slowly curved her long leg forward, moved Camille to slide along sweat-slicked skin to hold her, kiss her and tease resplendent after-shocks from her.

They made love in the spirited night until satiation and exhaustion claimed them, and a pale light of dawn found them wrapped in the warm secure press of each other's flesh.

"You're traveling with the show, aren't you?" Camille asked, turning to snuggle closer to Jessie.

"Yes. Why?" Jessie replied, sneaking a peek at her watch. it was five o'clock and she'd have to be with her crew all too soon.

"I was just wondering. Could there be any way I might persuade you to stay around . . . a while or longer?"

"Oh." Jessie let her gaze linger on Camille. "You've got plenty with which to charm me and it is a pretty idea. But this outfit's my chance at a decent-paying job."

"Well, you said you were a mechanic and could get anything to running. And I know that's right," Camille smiled wickedly.

"Your point being?" Jessie chuckled.

"I've got a farm. I inherited it from my folks. Large farm and ranch, actually. I recently fired the guy who was my manager."

"You want me to be a ranch hand?"

"No, I'd just like to have you there. With me. There's a lot of equipment, machinery and vehicles that need to be kept running. It'd keep you busy and time would let us know what else we might share."

"I don't know. Why don't we see how things go this week," Jessie stalled. "Give you time to change your mind. No fault, no blame," she offered chivalrously.

"Now, don't be stubborn. Remember, I know how to deal with stubborn," Camille cautioned, pulling Jessie to her. She stilled the protest on Jessie's lips by covering them with her own.

On Sunday night high southwest winds swept across the plains and scattered debris through the deserted fairgrounds. Jessie headed her truck out of town. She looked over at the sweetheart of the rodeo sitting beside her and felt her heart surge recklessly. She smiled at Camille as they drove toward the setting of the sun and home.

By the Light of the Moon
Marianne K. Martin

Johanna absently acknowledged and returned good-morning greetings along the wide sandy path from the camp office to her cabin. As she walked, she eagerly shuffled through the stack of mail, all addressed to Camp of the Council Fires, until she found the small envelope with her name on it. In an instant it was open.

Beautiful thief, you've stolen the breath from my lungs — left me desperate, powerless, except to wait for its return. And so I wait — for your smile, the sound of your voice, an unknowing look — while you steal away more than my breath.

She reached for the screen door of the cabin and with a smile welcomed the mysterious greeting in a familiar place, high above the handle. There, with a thread-like stem woven into the screen, was a tiny flower of the deepest purple, its feathery leaves so delicate they quivered in the wake of her breath. She plucked it carefully from the screen, and amidst the stirring of seven-year-olds, she placed it with the others in the vitamin-bottle vase next to her bunk.

"This is getting serious," Ginny grinned, pulling the last of their little charges from her bunk. "You're telling me you *still* have no idea who this could be? How many letters have you gotten now?"

"Four . . . and they're notes."

"Sent through the U.S. Postal Service, postmarked Traverse City . . . they're letters — love letters."

"I have no idea. But I've evidently reached my curiosity threshold. I'm ready to elicit your investigative skills." She acknowledged Ginny's excited gleam. "But you have to swear on your rainbow tattoo to keep this to yourself."

"Sworn." Ginny laughed, pledging with her hand over her left buttock.

They hustled their brood of sleepy-eyed campers through their morning tasks, and led them off to the main cabin for breakfast. Between bites, Johanna coaxed withdrawn little Mandy, starved more for attention than food, into eating the last of her oatmeal, and talked Lisa out of a third stack of pancakes that she shouldn't and really couldn't eat. Then, as Ginny "horsengoggled" to see who would claim the remaining sticky-bun, Johanna surveyed the faces of the staff. Thirty women, and three token men, in charge of 230 little girls for the duration of the summer. She realized that the possibility of someone outside the camp being responsible for the letters, and someone else *in* camp sending the flowers, was highly unlikely. And the chances of the flowers being for Ginny, of simultaneous suitors, was also unlikely. And these were not the words of a camper:

> *The mere thought of you lifts, as if on angels' wings, the weight of a lonely heart. And I thank you.*

She concentrated on the Head Table. Camp administrators, Head Counselor, Head of Waterfront, the men — everyone who held positions without campers. *Where to begin?* She'd already separated the singles from the married, the straights from the lesbians. But there were new counselors, and old ones about whom she could only make assumptions. And there were none of the usual signs from any of them — no looks that stayed too long, or wandered out-of-bounds, nobody spending too much time, or staying too close. Not that she had noticed, anyway. *That's* why she needed Ginny, the camp's self-appointed social director.

* * * * *

They sat on the cabin steps, speaking in quiet tones; the children were on their bunks, reading and writing letters. "Okay, I've eliminated everyone I think I can," Johanna concluded. "What can you tell me about the others?"

"Arts and Crafts is a 'het' — some strange relationship with an old hippie. Riding gave up on you last summer — she's dating the new counselor in the Cabin of Corn. The new sailing instructor doesn't fit with the Baywatch Bunch — she's the C.T. counselor's new love."

"Sharone is straight, right?"

"That's 'Don't *fuck* with me, I'm straight' Sharone," she emphasized. "She runs a tight waterfront, though . . . Too bad. Not for *me,*" she added quickly. "She's too feminine. But our diplomat the Head Counselor would wade ankle-deep into dead fishflies and shovel 'em bare-handed for the woman. I watched her last summer — it was painful. Oh, and don't forget the men." Johanna hung her head and groaned. "The new bugler is single, and of course John was divorced last year . . . You'd better hope it's Jan, and she's over Sharone."

"I don't know how you extract so much information. You're a walking personnel directory."

"I don't spend my days off in a movie theater," Ginny teased, raising her eyebrows.

"Yes, and we're *both* single. Or needn't I remind you?"

"I'm on hiatus."

"Of course, what was I thinking? So, what can we

deduce from this treasure trove of fascinating love-lore?"

"Maybe not as much as the letters themselves. If you'd let me read them, I might be of more help."

Johanna broke eye contact. The words whispered through her mind.

> *There was a time when I lost the light of the moon, and wandered helplessly, fearing even the night that had been my only solace. And now, I've found the light again in your eyes.*

She shook her head. "They weren't intended to be shared. They're something very personal, drawn from the person's heart. I would feel awful if they ever knew I gave them up for crass analysis."

Ginny rested a wedge of shiny dark hair in the palm of her hand, leaned her elbow on the top step and offered an expression that seemed to say, "So, what more can *I* do?"

Johanna opted for compromise. "They're not long flowery, sickening clichés of adoration. They're thoughts — feelings — that might occur suddenly, impulsively. Or they may have grown over a period of time and needed to be spoken, to be set free."

"Then you're more or less convinced that this isn't some sort of challenge thing, or an 'I'm bored out of my gourd' summer game."

"I may not bet the farm, as my dad would say, but I'd probably throw in the title to the family car." She lowered her eyes thoughtfully, a furrow forming between her brows. "It *does* put me in mind of something I did in high school, though." Ginny listened intently. "My best friend and I wrote notes during our last semester to this one teacher, Ms. Smythe, one of those teachers no one liked. Crotchety, burned-out, pitifully lonely, we decided. We wrote corny things like, 'I know this is a love that can never be,' and put them in her mailbox two or three times a week. The transformation was miraculous. She began to smile, fixed her hair, complimented her classes. We felt, in our humble anonymity, like angels. God, I hope *that's* not what this is all about!"

"*Please,* Johanna! You're 'over' and you know it." Ginny looked at her. "Look at yourself, for God's sake. In the three years I've known you, I've seen more suitors pursuing the enticingly elusive dance teacher than I can count on fingers and toes. That you choose to ignore most of them is *your* problem."

Johanna offered a bright smile. "I haven't found the right combination yet." More truthfully, it was love she hadn't found — the lose-all-sense-of-time, breath-catching kind of love that doesn't have to make sense. Oh, she'd loved all right, and been loved, in that initial curiosity of deflowering the mystery of another — the physical and mental exploration that eventually gives way to little vacancies in emotion that widen quickly into fissures too deep to fill with sex, or promises.

"Yeah, well, just keep in mind that getting romance and a good body is someone's idea of a cruel joke. I hope you haven't fallen into *that* fantasy trap. You know, you'd probably be better off if you never knew who this mystery romantic is. That way, when

real life becomes a bit too much, you'd always have
your fantasy lover to escape with."

Johanna shook her head with a friendly frown.
"You're so cynical."

"Oh, come on. This whole thing has you losing
sight of what we both know too well."

"And I'm sure you're about to remind me of what
that is."

"Someone has to," Ginny said as Johanna waited
with resolve. "True romantics die at age eight and
are reborn at sixty. And in between, there are jocks
with great bodies, whose ideas of romance are your
watching them play softball and drinking beer
afterwards . . . Face it, it's our destiny."

Destiny, Johanna thought. How differently we all
see it. Waiting, sometimes impatiently, for the powers
that be to pick up the next piece of the puzzle and
fit it neatly in place on their card table of a universe. Wasn't it *all* only an unfolding mystery? Like
her mystery lover's emerging butterfly?

> *In early-morning solitude, something stirs
> within my chest — the turnings of the butterfly
> against its cocoon of spun-tight threads — a
> heart preparing new wings for predestined
> flight.*

From her bunk, she stared out the window into
the magnitude of stars and felt suddenly very light
and small, as if all or part of her were being lifted
into the eternal recesses of space. Then a soft whim-

per escaped from a little camper's dream, and Johanna was suddenly back on solid ground. Although her mind was refreshingly clear, she realized she was no closer to identifying her mystery writer than she was three weeks ago.

Attempts to stay up all night to witness the delivery of the flower had failed; the flower appeared instead after they'd returned from breakfast. Questions, asked of campers in nearby cabins, produced no sightings of anyone else at the cabin door. Even comparing the handwriting to those on the sign-out sheets in the office had proved futile. Masterfully disguised penmanship, she wondered, or a dedicated counselor who sacrifices days off?

She laid the small pieces of stationery neatly on the wooden sill and, by the light of the moon, read them carefully again. The last one she had received only today.

> *Can love be the fire that warms my soul at the very sight of you? Is it the serenity that comes to me on air of midnight blue, from lullabies in the night? And too, the fear that chills my heart's courage at the thought of telling you? The questions that furrow my worried brow have written their marks upon my soul. Is it insanity, or love, that drives me mad?*

Suddenly, the emotions of the words began rushing her mind, flooding her with feeling. Feelings pouring from words spoken to her in naked honesty.

An honesty of emotion that had no face, no body, nothing to detract from it, nothing to hide it. Yet it had a presence so overwhelming that she found herself filled with a strange excitement. Was it possible to fall in love with someone and not even know who it was? The thumping in her chest spoke a language so universal not even Johanna could mistake its answer. She began reading the notes once again, shaking her head in wonderment.

As she gathered the papers, a still-folded sheet slipped from today's envelope. In her haste earlier in the day, it had gone unnoticed. She held it in the moonlight and read.

> *If it is ever your wish that my attention stop, you need only to close the shutter above your cabin sign, and I will understand. Otherwise, when your heart is sure it seeks not out of curiosity, you will find me where the light of the moon looks down upon its own beauty . . . and I will know.*

Quickly she looked to the shutter and to her relief found it open. Yes, she thought anxiously, I will find you.

All day she searched the faces again, each one while the words played through her mind, trying to make the pieces fit. But still she saw nothing. Finally, with the children settled in their bunks for the night, she motioned Ginny to the door. She showed her the last message. "What are you going to do?" Ginny asked in a whisper.

"See if I can find her."

"Or him? What if it's a man?"

"If it's a man, he has the soul of a woman."

"Do you want my opinion?"

"Do I have a choice?"

"Shut the damn shutter and forget it. This could be Quasimodo courting you. Are you ready to find *that* out?"

"Whoever it is, they're beautiful where it counts."

"The beauty and her beast." Ginny shook her head in resignation. "Go on then, get out of here. I have the cabin covered. Go search out your beast."

"Shhhh, not so loud," Johanna whispered, dabbing cologne under the collar of her shirt. "I'll have a safari of seven-year-olds begging to follow me, and you'll be ghost-busting nightmares for the rest of them."

Ginny moved a step closer and whispered, "I might suggest a kitchen raid first . . . in case it hasn't eaten in a while. A little cheesecake, maybe?" She grinned.

"Stop it!" she chided, raising her whisper to its limit. "You're awful."

Johanna backed out the door and smiled as the questions began. "Where's Johanna going?" small voices asked. Serves her right! And they'll be wanting a lullaby tonight, too.

She walked the length of camp, beyond the lighted paths, finding herself climbing the hill over-

looking the grounds. Streaks of moonlight, penetrating the canopy of maple and pine, shone in spots
along the dark wooded path. From the clearing at the
top, open to the full illumination of the moon, she
looked down upon the camp. Paths, like golden
fingers of light, stretched from a bright palm of sand,
each to a little darkened cabin. The gray-green of the
tennis court lay under splashes of moon-cast shadows,
and a lone lighted window, like a watchful eye, shone
from the owner's quarters. Then she saw it. Between
stands of stately pine, glimmering in majesty across
the rippled surface, the moon cast reflected beauty
upon the lake. *Where the light of the moon looks
down upon its own beauty.*

Her heart beat ardently in anticipation. She
rushed back down the dark path and hurried quietly
through camp. From atop the little knoll above the
beach she surveyed the shoreline; all was still, but
for the naked masts of the sailboats bobbing and
swaying in the swelling water. Then a movement
caught her eye, halfway down the boat dock. But it
was only Sharone, dark braid hanging down her back,
checking the moorings of the boats as the wind
kicked up over the lake. Satisfied that all was secure,
she disappeared moments later into the shadows
toward her cabin.

Johanna waited, watchful, anxious for the one
whose words had aroused her sleeping heart. Somehow she knew it wouldn't be long. She stepped
slowly down the sandy knoll and onto the beach. She
tilted back her head, breathed in the cooling wind
from the lake, while the riggings clanged restlessly
against the masts.

"Don't turn around yet, please," came a voice, soft as a wind through white pine. A voice she knew. "There's something I need to say."

Johanna's heart jumped, and she closed her eyes in relief at the sound of the woman's voice.

"I understand that your being here may be merely curiosity." The voice drew nearer; its presence felt close behind. "For three years I've been afraid of these growing feelings for you . . ." Warm currents traveled quickly from the fingers touching the top of Johanna's hand, bringing glorious warmth throughout her body. "Because I know I'm not the kind of woman you're —"

"Attracted to," she said as she turned, sparked with electricity, and looked into Sharone's eyes.

Sharone's breath stopped with a catch. "Yes," she said, very softly. "I thought if you saw me from the inside first . . ."

"That I'd be able to overlook how visibly beautiful you are?" While she began melting under Sharone's loving gaze, Johanna slowly shook her head. "No, sweet woman, it can't be, won't be overlooked. Not any longer. Nor can the fact that your eyes are doing to me what your words have done all summer."

Johanna took her hand and held it as Sharone spoke. "It's always been so hard for others to see me for who I am. Love never seemed to have a chance."

Sharone's fingers gently captured windblown strands of her hair and tucked them carefully back in place. Johanna smiled at the stirring it caused in her chest. *The butterfly opening new wings.* She reached for Sharone's hand, held it for a second against her hair, then pressed her lips into the soft palm. "Love

is born of the heart," she whispered. "And mine" —
she drew Sharone's hand over her heart — "may have
already fallen in love with yours."

The lips that touched her now, grazed across her
own with such tender affection, magnetized her as no
others had. The arms steadying their embrace roused
her body immediately to full sensitivity. Johanna slid
her fingers through raven silk hair, set free of its
braid, and opened her lips, as she had her heart.
Wholly and unconditionally, she brought Sharone's
love within. Glowing with desire in the arms of her
mystery woman, she marveled at how clearly one can
see by the light of the moon.

Doctor's Orders
Frankie J. Jones

Callie Peterson moaned and brushed the irritating fly from her cheek. The cool breeze and steady sway of the boat lulled her back into the cotton-soft cocoon of sleep. Then a sharp stinging sensation brought her fully awake. She sat up and scratched her chin where the fly had stung her.

"Damn. I hate bugs," she growled as she pulled her lanky body upright.

Callie had been hired by Dr. Irene Givens, a prominent botanist, to ferry her to the far side of

Lake Owens. Givens was studying a rare species of fern that had recently been discovered growing in this remote region. The fern had been spotted by Ralph Mitchell, a hunter who happened to be an amateur botanist. Callie couldn't understand all the uproar about a fern, but her fee was the same regardless and Givens had been more than willing to charter the boat for an entire day.

Callie noticed the dark clouds forming on the horizon. They should be returning to town. She didn't relish the thought of being caught on the open lake in a thunderstorm. She glanced at her watch and noted that Dr. Givens was already late in returning. Normally this wasn't a problem; Callie would simply add the additional time to the bill, but the storm clouds worried her. She contemplated going to look for Givens as a long, jagged spear of lightning flashed in the distance. Callie strained to hear the thunder, but the storm was too far away. Not knowing exactly where Givens had gone, she decided to wait a few minutes before beginning her search. They would probably end up missing each other anyway, since Dr. Givens had only given her the briefest description of where she was going.

Callie set about securing the loose items that always seemed to accumulate whenever passengers were on board. In the twelve years that she had operated Peterson's Charter Service, Callie had dealt with all kinds of people. Her least favorite were those like Irene Givens — people so bent on their own quest that they had no time for those around them. Givens had spent the entire two-hour trip with her nose in a book.

"Probably sleeps with a book," Callie grumbled. She pushed the sour thoughts away, knowing they dealt more with the recent disintegration of her five-year relationship with Judy than with this unknown woman's personality.

Judy had been self-centered and distant. At first Callie had thought Judy would change as they got to know each other better. She had hoped that Judy would open up to her, but Judy didn't change and they had slowly and painfully drifted apart. At least it was painful for Callie. She still wasn't sure how Judy felt.

Callie shrugged the tenseness from her shoulders and again studied the storm clouds that pushed steadily nearer. She had to get Givens out of there or they would be forced to ride out the storm on the boat. She glanced toward the heavily timbered shore-line where Dr. Givens had disappeared hours earlier.

"Would I even be able to find her?" Callie wondered aloud. A long roll of thunder persuaded her that she had to at least try.

The rain began as Callie entered the woods. The wind tugged at the tree branches above her. Instinct told her she had waited too long. She shivered as a cold trickle of rainwater ran down her collar.

"Dr. Givens!" she called again and again to no avail. The wind howled as thunder boomed jarring the ground beneath her. Callie eyed the swaying tree limbs with trepidation and pushed through the under-brush while debating whether or not to continue. It would be easy for them to miss each other in the dense growth of trees. The storm escalated in its intensity and the woods grew darker.

A thin finger of panic began to pluck at her. Suppose she got lost and couldn't find her way back to the boat? She was at home on the open water, not in these smothering woods. Callie broke into a run, screaming for Dr. Givens, but the roaring wind ripped the sound away from her. A wicked streak of lightning flashed just as she tore through a clump of thick underbrush and ran into a drenched Dr. Givens.

"What the hell are you still doing out here?" Callie screamed in an effort to hide her own terror as much as to express her anger with Dr. Givens. "Don't you know how dangerous this is?"

"I'm not stupid!" Dr. Givens snapped, brushing a wet strand of her dark hair away from her equally dark eyes. "The storm came up before I realized it!" Her eyes blazed and for the briefest instant Callie was held by their intensity.

"We've got to get back to the boat!" Callie pulled her gaze away and shouted above the howling wind. A large limb broke loose from a dead tree nearby and crashed to the ground. Callie turned to go back to the boat, but the woman grabbed her arm. "Come on!" Callie shrieked, trying to control her fear.

"The cabin is much closer."

"What cabin?" Callie screamed, staring around them at the whipping trees.

Without waiting to answer, Dr. Givens yanked Callie's arm with such force that she had no choice but to follow or fall. They pushed their way through a dense mass of vines and other vegetation until Callie was lost beyond hope. She knew she'd never be able to find the boat by herself. She had no option now but to follow.

The tangled jumble of roots and fallen limbs commanded Callie's full attention. She was caught off guard when Dr. Givens stopped abruptly. Callie plowed into her, sending them both to the ground.

"I'm sorry," Callie began as she tried to stand.

Arms encircled her, halting her struggle. Callie could feel the other woman's soft breasts and the strength of her arms. She found herself unable to look away from the dark eyes that boldly challenged. For the briefest moment Callie allowed herself to enjoy the feeling, before remembering what a blundering fool she'd been. In her embarrassment it took Callie a moment to realize they were no longer in the rain but lying in the doorway of a small cabin. She moved and the arms released her. Callie tried to ignore the sharp stab of disappointment.

"This is Ralph's hunting lodge," Dr. Givens explained, interrupting Callie's thoughts as they began the untangling of bodies. Callie stood aside, confused by her reaction to this remote woman.

"He told me where it was when he called to report his discovery." Dr. Givens closed the door and began searching the darkened shelves. "There should be a lantern or a lamp of some kind. There's no electricity up here. Not that it would matter in this storm."

Callie continued to watch as the woman pulled a lantern down from a shelf.

"I'm sure there are matches here somewhere," she said, digging through cabinet drawers. Callie realized that Dr. Givens was as flustered by their encounter as she was. This knowledge gave her the courage to move toward the huge fireplace that filled one end

wall of the cabin. She found the matches in a metal
tea tin.

"Here they are," she said. Taking the matches she
walked to where Givens held the lantern. Callie found
she was still very much aware of the other woman's
presence.

Dr. Givens held the globe up while Callie lit the
lantern with trembling fingers. *It's the cold*, she told
herself and stepped quickly away when the wick
caught.

"I'll get a fire started," Callie offered. She knelt
before the fireplace where a large supply of wood lay
waiting. She focused on building the fire. Never had
any fire received so much of her undivided attention,
but still it dimmed in comparison to the fire that Dr.
Irene Givens had ignited within her.

"I found some coffee."

Callie jumped at the sound of the voice beside
her. She had been so lost in her thoughts she hadn't
heard her approach. She watched as Dr. Givens set
the pot on a grill near the flames.

"I didn't mean to frighten you," Dr. Givens apologized as she stood.

"You didn't . . . um . . . I was . . ." A hand on her
arm stopped her.

"We've got to get out of these wet clothes before
we catch pneumonia," Dr. Givens said.

Callie felt a stampede of butterflies invade her
stomach as the woman's dark eyes again captured
her.

"Take your clothes off and I'll find you a blanket
to wrap up in," Givens said, holding Callie's gaze for

another moment before going to the nearby bed and removing a blanket.

Callie struggled to control her breathing and fumbled with her shirt buttons, but her fingers seemed to have forgotten how to act.

"You're freezing. Let me help." Dr. Givens folded the blanket over her own shoulder and slowly began to unbutton Callie's shirt. Unable to meet those haunting dark eyes again, Callie focused her attention on the bright patterns on the blanket. She heard her own sharp intake of breath as Dr. Givens' fingertips gently brushed against the bare skin of her stomach.

A thousand thoughts ran through Callie's mind, but none of them lingered long enough for her to grasp. All she could do was stand there in a daze as the woman eased the sopping shirt back off Callie's shoulders.

"You're very beautiful," she murmured as her hands trailed down Callie's back, pushing away the wet shirt.

Callie felt her nipples grow rigid. *It's the cold air*, she told herself again.

Callie had been in two previous relationships and she had been the instigator in both. Never had anyone been so blatantly obvious in expressing desire for her.

"Why don't we get rid of these?" Dr. Givens whispered as her fingers slid behind the first button of Callie's jeans.

Callie raised her eyes to find the woman watching her intently, a small smile shadowing the corner of her mouth.

"If this isn't what you want, you can say stop at any time," Dr. Givens said, tugging the second button on Callie's jeans free.

"How could I possibly say no to what you're doing?" Callie asked, finding her voice at last.

Dr. Givens chuckled. "Simply tell me to be good and I'll wrap you in this warm blanket."

Callie's hands slid to Dr. Givens' hips and pulled her tightly against her. The sodden slacks were cold to Callie's touch. "Be good and wrap the blanket around both of us," she said, lowering her head to trace her lips lightly along the doctor's neck. Warmth shot through her at the sound of the other woman's deep moan. Callie turned her head and their lips merged in a rush of desire.

Callie freed the buttons from Dr. Givens' shirt while her lips continued their slow feast. Never had she wanted anyone so desperately. Her jeans were shoved from her hips and an urgent hand slid between her legs.

Callie heard herself moan as long cool fingers parted her burning desire and began a slow stroking motion that caused Callie's knees to weaken.

"I can't stand any longer," she managed to gasp as the fingers slid deep within her. Callie felt herself being guided toward the bed. Strong arms leaned her back and a warm pliant body covered her. Callie tried to remember how Dr. Givens had gotten undressed, but the fingers inside her were becoming more insistent. A warm mouth covered an aching nipple and Callie felt herself falling into a whirling mass of sensations.

When Callie could again breathe, she rolled them

over until she was staring down into those hypnotic eyes. "Dr. Givens, you have beautiful eyes," she whispered, letting her lips graze across a cheek and along her ear.

"Considering the events of the last few minutes maybe you should call me Irene," she answered in a voice tinted with amusement.

Callie leaned on one elbow to peer down at her. "Is that what the doctor orders?" she asked, teasing a damp curl away from Irene's forehead.

"Do you always follow doctor's orders?" Irene asked with a wicked smile.

"Always," Callie insisted. Her hand captured a soft full breast and began to knead the already taut nipple.

"In that case," Irene said, pulling Callie's head down to whisper in her ear.

Callie felt her heart leap and a new wave of heat flare within her as she listened to vivid details of what was being requested of her. These were certainly one set of doctor's orders she would follow with pleasure.

Dykes in Space

Peggy J. Herring

Having already said good-bye to her friends, Lieutenant Pastel boarded the shuttle that would take her away from what she had called home for the past eighteen months. Out of the dozen or so women stationed on the rock with her, some of them Pastel would miss terribly, while others she truly hoped never to see again.

As the Executive Officer of a very remote communications outpost, Lieutenant Pastel had learned a lot during her eighteen-month tour. She was a better

officer for being here and had confidence in her
newly acquired skills. Pastel's replacement had arrived
on the same shuttle that was now ready to whisk her
away to the Mother Base where she would have a
whole week to readjust to being back from deep
space. She still found it hard to believe that she was
leaving this place, and in a way it seemed almost
impossible that her time on the rock was over.

While the pilot made sure everyone was ade-
quately secure in their sleeping compartments, Pastel
wondered briefly if she would dream about Dakota
again. Even though she'd spent a good portion of the
last year and a half trying to forget her, dreams
about their time together still came to her often. No
one but Dakota had ever affected her this way, and
Pastel had hoped that she'd be over this obsession
long before now, but so far it hadn't happened.

Pastel and Dakota had been lovers for only a few
weeks when they were abruptly reassigned to different locations. If Pastel's orders for an executive
officer's position had been a surprise, then Dakota's
promotion to Commandant of the Academy, making
her the third in command of the Star Fleet, had
been absolutely mind-boggling. Overnight Dakota had
gone from commanding a rescue ship with a crew of
five to Academy Commandant where she was responsible for training all Star Fleet cadets. There had
been no one better for the job, of course, and Dakota
was an excellent choice for such a prestigious position. She had impeccable military bearing and
brought out the best in subordinates, demanding
nothing less than a top performance from each and

every one. But for Pastel, her time with Dakota had been too short.

On their final day together, they were issued different uniforms and given a comfortable room for the remainder of their one-hour stay at the Mother Base. As soon as they were alone in their room, Dakota asked Pastel if she was feeling all right.

"I'm fine," Pastel said. She let Dakota take her by the hand and lead her to the bed. "Everything's changing so fast," she said. "We'll never be stationed together again. The most we can hope for is a chance meeting somewhere."

"Come here," Dakota whispered. She took Pastel in her arms and hugged her. "You have to trust me. I want more than that too."

Thinking was definitely getting in the way, Pastel decided. She was ready to forgo the doom and gloom of the future for a few final blissful moments with the woman she loved. She gently tugged on Dakota's uniform and began taking it off of her. Dakota's hand touched Pastel's cheek and then slipped behind her head to bring her closer for a slow, deep kiss. Pastel immediately became lost in sensation. Dakota's mouth was soft and possessive, and her darting tongue sent a surge of desire coursing through Pastel's body. She trembled in response and pressed Dakota down on the bed. *You'll never see her again after this,* she thought. *Never.*

Dakota kissed Pastel's throat and bare shoulder, but the need to be even closer seemed to come over them both at the same time. They were a tangled mass of arms and legs, thriving on heat and desperation as they rolled around on the bed. Pastel's body throbbed with anticipation until Dakota finally ended up on top of her. She recognized the pure desire in Dakota's eyes and felt a rush of emotion as she reached up to take Dakota's face in her hands. *You'll never see her again after this . . .*

Dakota leaned closer to kiss her, and Pastel ached at just the thought of losing her. Why was this happening to them? Why now?

Dakota eased down Pastel's body and kissed everywhere as she went. Pastel finally stopped thinking long enough to let instinct take over. Their last time making love couldn't end this way.

"No," Pastel whispered. "Together. Please. Both at the same time." She raised up and slowly moved around on the bed. Her bare ankle felt the brush of Dakota's thick soft hair as they readjusted their positions, and without preamble Pastel buried her face and tongue between Dakota's open legs. *Like this,* she thought, savoring the taste of her as Dakota groaned her surprise and pleasure. *Like this. Together.* Seconds later Pastel's legs were urged apart and Dakota's mouth and tongue were on her, in her, sucking and probing greedily.

They came together in a sweaty heap of quivering flesh. Pastel eventually turned back around, kissing Dakota's thigh and hip as she went, and curled into her arms. Through the heavy silence that followed, they held each other until there was absolutely no more time left. In silence they untangled themselves and began getting dressed, careful not to touch each other again.

Pastel kept her thoughts to herself until Dakota

finally asked her how many women were stationed at
the outpost she was being transferred to. "Fourteen,"
Pastel replied. "Why?"

Dakota didn't answer, but Pastel could see that
there was more she wanted to say. *She's jealous,*
Pastel thought suddenly. *What's going on here?*

"How many cadets are at the Academy?" Pastel
asked after a moment.

"It isn't the same thing."

"Why not?" She pulled on a new gray boot with
more force than was called for. "Three hundred
female cadets with raging hormones. Not to mention
a staff of fifty lesbians panting after you."

"Panting?" Dakota said with a raised eyebrow.
"There won't be any panting."

Pastel zipped up her new flight suit and ran her
fingers through her blonde hair. "Let's not talk about
it anymore, okay?" *Why are we doing this? Why are
we arguing our last few minutes together?* Pastel
wanted to leave before she started to cry.

Dakota touched her arm and turned her around.
"I'm in love with you," she said, her voice breaking.

"Please don't say it," Pastel whispered. "Not
now."

"I have to."

Pastel kissed her quickly then stepped back and
leaned against the door. "I've gotta go. My shuttle's
waiting."

"Pastel —"

"And you're expected in the Command Suite for a
briefing in two minutes. You'd better hurry."

"I'll be here when you come back," Dakota said.
"In eighteen months. I'll be here waiting for you."

Pastel turned away from her and was out the door and down the corridor while she still had the strength to do it. Leaving her was the hardest thing she'd ever done, and Pastel felt numb and drained as each step took her farther and farther away. She held fast to the hope that her new job would keep her too busy to dwell on any of this, but eighteen months suddenly seemed like forever. She'd made her decision and now she had to live with it.

And so it went, just as Pastel had expected. Her first few weeks on the rock were predictable, but even though there was a lot to learn, she welcomed the distraction. At night, alone in her room, she'd lie awake on her hard, tiny bunk and think about Dakota and their time together, but Pastel knew she couldn't continue doing that — she'd be nuts in a month at that rate. So she worked long hours and volunteered for extra duty in addition to her regular job as the Executive Officer. As a result, she quickly became a favorite of the crew, who were more than willing to take advantage of her desire to stay busy. Most nights Pastel was even too tired to notice the low moans seeping through the thin walls of the compound, or to acknowledge the sexual offers and innuendoes often tossed in her direction. Work had finally helped her forget, and forgetting had made being there much easier.

Through a veil of sleep, Pastel vaguely heard the pilot announce their arrival. The top of her sleeping compartment slowly opened and she squeezed her eyes shut and yawned. Pastel heard the hum of the Mother Base while her groggy head began to clear, and she realized that they'd picked up four additional passengers along the way.

"Don't forget to check the directory," the pilot informed them.

Pastel glanced at the console near the pilot's seat and wondered if Dakota's name would be there. The directory was automatically updated whenever someone either arrived at or departed from the Mother Base compound. Friends, old lovers and classmates could easily be located, and much of everyone's time at the Mother Base was usually spent with someone they knew.

Pastel watched the four passengers rush to the console, but she wasn't in a hurry to move yet. *Is Dakota's name listed?* she wondered. *Is she here like she promised she'd be?*

Reliving her last few minutes with Dakota — a time that would be forever etched in her mind — Pastel closed her eyes and took a deep breath. The queasiness in her stomach returned the moment she opened her eyes again and looked at the console. As the four chattering passengers made plans for their stay at the Mother Base, Pastel could hear the excitement in their voices. She got up and stretched, stalling for time. *If her name's not there I could just catch up on sleep,* she thought reasonably, *or maybe they'll let me report to my new assignment early.*

Squeals of delight erupted through the control room before the door swooshed open and the four passengers departed. Pastel stood there staring at the console, torn between wanting to know and *not* wanting to know if Dakota's name would appear there.

"Most people I pick up from the rock are very happy to be here," the pilot said with a laugh. She was about Pastel's height and age and had short red hair and a nice smile. "You must've left someone important behind. Remote assignments are always hard on the heart."

"True," Pastel said quietly, having nothing further to add.

"You haven't checked the directory yet," the pilot reminded her.

Pastel considered ignoring her but didn't want to draw more attention to herself. She nervously cleared her throat and finally let her gaze settle on the console where the directory waited. *Go ahead and look. Get it over with. If she's not here, then you can sleep, drink and cry for a week.*

"Are you looking for anyone in particular?" the pilot asked, nodding toward the directory. "Check it out. You might be surprised."

Pastel reached for her helmet in the sleeping compartment and walked to the console. She pushed a button and watched as the names began a slow scroll up and off the screen. Dakota's name wasn't there.

"So much for surprises," she said, biting her lower lip. She couldn't believe how disappointed she felt. *In the back of your mind you actually thought she'd be waiting for you here, didn't you?*

"Sounds like a trip to the cantina's in order," the pilot said heartily. "Maybe we could spend some time together."

"I won't be very good company. Thanks anyway."
Pastel wanted to be somewhere else — *anywhere* else
right then. The cabin door swooshed open and she
found herself in the huge corridor leading away from
the loading dock. The low hum of the Mother Base,
which was specifically designed to soothe and relax,
had very little effect on her. Pastel tucked her helmet
under her arm and made a decision. She would report to the personnel office and request to leave early
for her new assignment. *The sooner you're out of here
the better.*

She looked at the glowing map on the wall and
tried to find the shortest route to personnel from
where she was. *What made you think you could stay
here without her? You've got too many memories of
this place.*

The Mother Base was a vast resort tailored for
those who were tired and weary from the rigors of
space travel and lengthy remote assignments. It was
a playground where relaxation took precedence over
everything else. Pastel was too upset to relax, even
though she knew that if she stayed her allotted seven
days, she would probably eventually feel better. For
that reason alone, the Star Fleet personnel office
might not approve her request to leave early.

"Lieutenant Pastel?" a voice behind her called.

Pastel glanced back over her shoulder and met
the woman's questioning look. She wore Security
insignia on her collar and the rank of Major, but
Pastel had never seen her before.

"I'm Major Striker," the woman said. "Security
Advisor for the Academy."

Pastel noticed the rest of her uniform for the first

time — a gray flight suit with gold brocade running along the outside seams. A thin black sash draped over one shoulder had the Academy emblem on it.

The Academy. She's from the Academy. Pastel could feel the tension easing from her body almost immediately. "Dakota sent you."

Striker smiled. "Yes. Dakota sent me."

Pastel felt renewed excitement at just hearing Dakota's name. "Where is she?"

"Unfortunately she's still at the Academy. Something's come up, and she can't get away right now."

"But she wants to see me," Pastel said. She needed everything clear in her head right now. This was not the time for a misunderstanding.

"Oh, yes," Striker said. "She definitely wants to see you."

Pastel put her helmet on. "Then take me to her." She watched as Striker's eyes widened in surprise, but there was no resistance. Striker motioned toward a spidercraft across the cargo bay — the only aircraft in the area with the Academy emblem on it. They crawled inside and Striker punched in several coordinates, getting them on their way. Once they were en route, Pastel looked over at her and asked, "How is she? Tell me everything."

"Before we get into any of that, I need to ask you a question first," Striker said. "We only found out about you last week. Needless to say the Academy's buzzing with rumors and curiosity."

"What's your question?"

Striker flexed her hand and nervously tugged at a tight glove. "If a position at the Academy were to be offered to you, would you take it?"

Pastel's heart began thumping away as she leaned her head back and closed her eyes. She'd thought about this a thousand times since she'd been away.

"If your answer is no," Striker said quietly, "then I'm returning you to the Mother Base immediately. I won't have Dakota upset over this. I'll just tell her that you chose to spend your time somewhere else and she can draw her own conclusions from that."

It didn't occur to Pastel to inquire about the type of position being offered, or the likelihood of any promotion potential. All she could think about right then was being with Dakota again.

"Well, Lieutenant?" Striker said. "Yes or no? If one were offered would you accept a position with us?"

"Yes," Pastel said, not recognizing her own voice. She cleared her throat and said with a bit more conviction, "Of course I would." She stared straight ahead, still stunned by this sudden turn of events. Was Dakota planning to find a legitimate place for her at the Academy? *Or will you merely be the Commandant's lover and nothing more?*

"Dakota deserves only the best," Striker said, looking at her long and hard. "A lot will be expected of you if you stay."

With more confidence than she actually felt at the moment, Pastel returned the look and said, "I know better than anyone what Dakota likes and wants, Major. Trust me on that."

The remainder of the forty-five-minute trip was spent in silence until Striker requested permission to enter Academy air space.

"Permission granted," came the efficient voice into

their helmets. "Excellent, Striker. You found her. We'll try to have the Commandant on deck by the time you get here."

The Commandant, Pastel thought as a surge of uneasiness soared through her. *Is Dakota still the same person you knew? How much has this job changed her?*

They approached the Academy's flight deck where everything was just as Pastel remembered it from her days as a cadet here. The only difference was the lack of people milling around. The cargo bay was deserted when ordinarily there should be shuttle crews and scores of cadets in various stages of training.

Striker set the spidercraft down gently and they both remained very still for a moment.

"How many of you are in love with her already?" Pastel asked.

Striker nodded and suppressed a smile. "A few," she admitted, "but at least now we know why Dakota's never been interested."

The door to the spidercraft hummed open and Pastel and Striker climbed out. Pastel saw Dakota standing alone beside a small transport. She looked the same — regal and imposing, jet-black hair touching her shoulders, well-defined cheekbones and dark, piercing eyes. She was beautiful.

Pastel took her helmet off and gave it to Striker automatically. Seeing the look in Dakota's eyes was all the reassurance Pastel needed. There was love and longing in Dakota's expression, and they were in each other's arms, lost in a deep, breathtaking kiss within seconds.

"I've missed you so much," Dakota said as she hugged her and buried her face in Pastel's neck. "You're really here. I was afraid Striker wouldn't find you."

Pastel laughed. "You gave me a good scare." Moments later they were kissing again, and Pastel filled her hands with Dakota's thick black hair. She heard that soft moan in Dakota's throat and felt a new surge of desire race through her.

"I'm one step away from tearing your clothes off," Pastel warned convincingly. Manic, erratic kisses followed and then Pastel tugged on Dakota's earlobe with her teeth. "Just one step away," she whispered.

The Lady Is a Tramp
Pat Welch

I still wasn't sure if I wanted to use a gun or a knife or some slow-acting poison that would make my victim suffer a painful, gruesome death.

"Would you like another drink?"

Smiling, I nodded and asked the waitress for a second Manhattan. Under normal circumstances, I would have requested a single glass of white wine. This situation, of course, was far from normal.

Besides, a quaint old-fashioned sort of cocktail matched the ambience. I'd never set foot in Anything

Goes before, but the happy-hour crowd testified to the bar's popularity. Lots of gleaming chrome, dark polished wood and the fog of cigarette smoke enveloped the patrons of the bar in a weird, fixed sepia glow. Gershwin tunes floated the gaiety. I glanced again at the wall to my left, where huge picture windows offered a spectacular view of the Golden Gate Bridge. They would have, that is, if the patrons weren't blocking my line of sight, keeping me from seeing the city lights twinkle on as the sun sank beyond San Francisco Bay.

I caught a sudden glance of myself reflected in the window. Although I was still five pounds heavier than I wanted to be, the black suit I'd chosen for this little tête-à-tête set off my thick blonde hair and pale skin. My husband always told me that black made me look like a minister's wife, but anything was better than appearing like the ignorant, dim-witted suburban housewife I was.

"Anything else?"

"No, thank you." I turned away from the waitress and picked up my drink. "Cheers."

The woman sitting across from me in the booth said nothing. I sipped and stared, letting the alcohol work its old black magic on me. By this time, Cheryl Evans was beginning to squirm on the red leather cushions. Odd — the bitch seemed to fit in this place quite well, with her Joan Crawford eyes and simple tailored suit. Those eyelashes, so long and thick, looked real. And the soft pink fingernails, too. They were just the right length, not too long and not too short. Cheryl tapped her glass with them, then ran one hand through the sleek black hair cropped close to her scalp. I sighed. My husband's taste in mistresses was definitely improving.

"Look, Mrs. Hammett —"

"Please, call me June."

Her lips — the lower one was slightly fuller than the upper one — pouted quite prettily as a grimace flickered across her face. "June, I know you didn't just invite me here for a drink. Not that I'm complaining. I've wanted to get to know you better."

She leaned forward. I couldn't help noticing how her breasts pressed up against her silk blouse, the cleavage deep and shadowed in the dim light. "For quite a long time, actually."

I wanted to slap her right then — wipe off that smile, make those dark unreadable eyes fill with tears. What the hell was this cozy little overture of friendship? Was I supposed to be deceived by that warmth flowing across the table to me? "I suppose making friends with your lover's wife is fashionable these days," I said, leaning back, away from her. In spite of my determination to project a stony rage, I heard my voice quaver. I reached for the brand new Manhattan and drank quickly, glad of the bitter heat from the drink that would cover the despair and hurt in my voice.

It was difficult to keep from staring at her. She looked so different from the first time I'd seen her — what was it — two years ago? The white pickup blazoned with the words EVANS LANDSCAPING — WE CAN DIG IT had first appeared in my neighborhood right after we moved into our new house. It was a big step for us, leaving the grime and crime of the city for our first suburban home. Of course, we'd both wanted the yard to look nice. That was why we'd hired the bitch in the first place. All the couples on our block raved about her work, even though they raised an eyebrow or two as they recommended her.

"So what's that weird look for?" I'd ask, watching my new neighbors smirk over their coffee. "Is there something about this Evans woman you're not telling me?"

"Oh, no, nothing! She's just — well, unusual. That's all. But good, really good at her job."

That was the best I could get out of any of them. I watched Cheryl closely for the first few days, feeling a bit ashamed but not wanting to be caught by surprise if she suddenly decided to steal the silver or take off with my shiny new kitchen appliances.

Dave watched, too. He'd bring home his work, slather his body with greasy sun block and park his horny little butt out on the patio, cell phone in one hand and a drink in the other, while no doubt the pile of papers in his lap hid a multitude of sins. I mean, at first I could hardly blame him. She'd wear some kind of halter top thing that showed her flat belly, and cut-off shorts revealed every flex of muscle in her legs as she raked and trimmed and dug and planted and pulled. All those Saturday afternoons, the sun beating down fiercely on her back and shoulders, the sweat gleaming and dripping across her golden skin.

I have to admit, though, she was cool. They both were. I mean, she'd barely speak to him while she worked — probably because she knew I was there, watching every move. He'd sit and stare from his chair while I stared from the kitchen window. She almost had me convinced she'd forgotten about his existence, then she'd turn those eyes to look right back at me, over Dave's balding head that glared in the sun.

That was when I knew. That look. Cheryl had stood up, her body gleaming as if she'd been dipped in syrup, gripped a spade so tightly with both hands that her knuckles shone pale through the layer of earth that coated her skin. She'd loosened one hand to run fingers through her sweat-soaked hair, slicking it back away from her eyes, her chest heaving as if she'd been running very hard and only just paused in flight.

It struck me, as I sat there watching her twist her glass around with nervous hands, that I'd never seen her cleaned up and dressed up before. Her simple suit, her large capable hands, did not dispel my memories of the way she looked when she'd labored in my backyard. I could still feel the heat in those eyes, radiating out to me from where she'd stood, spade in hand, watching. Watching and waiting.

And now those same eyes widened in astonishment. A fresh jolt of confidence flowed through me at the sight of her consternation. I forced a laugh and plunked my glass back onto the table.

"Oh, for God's sake, don't give me that look of surprise. We both know what's going on here." I very nearly did slap her then. She deserved an Oscar for those rounded eyes, the sharp gasp, the way her mouth fell open.

"Jesus Christ," she whispered, leaning back in the booth. "So that's — I mean, no wonder —"

"Just how stupid did you two think I was?"

Anger was finally taking over, and rage mixed with alcohol kicked in an extra bolus of pride. "All those phone calls late at night, pretending to talk to me when you really wanted to know if Dave was home, stopping by on weekends. Not to mention all those cute little presents Dave's been throwing my way." That Manhattan felt awfully good going down as I finished the last swallow. Maybe just one more would see me through this. "He finally admitted those presents were your idea. Even down to suggesting the colors on the scarf he brought home last week."

"An affair. Me and Dave."

Her laughter took me by surprise. I hadn't expected that. It wasn't a mean laugh, either — this sounded like delight, a real belly laugh.

"Well, I'm certainly glad someone is enjoying this."

She wiped her eyes, her body still shaking with suppressed hilarity. "Oh, Lord! I'm really sorry, June." A few more giggles spurted out. The waiter had reappeared, and I suddenly realized that an awful lot of eyes had glanced our way. "Yes, I'd like another. How about you, June? This round is on me."

Wait a damned minute. This was going all wrong. The barrage of alcohol I'd just subjected my body to began to roil around in my stomach. I'm not sure how long it took me to figure out my mouth was open, my jaw loose with surprise. I clamped my mouth shut and shook my head at the waiter, who scurried away after I glared at him.

By now Cheryl had stopped laughing. Thank God for the dim mood lighting — she wouldn't be able to see how my face burned. "I should have known

better," I mumbled, hoping my voice came out cool
and detached. "When they talked about you, I should
have picked up on the cues —"

"June, what the hell are you talking about?" she
asked in a voice that lilted with amusement.

"They all acted strange when I asked about you.
The neighbors, I mean. And I thought it was because
maybe you stole things. What a fucking fool I was."

Goddammit, I didn't need those wide green eyes
looking at me with — well, warmth, I guess. I didn't
know what else to call it.

When Cheryl reached out her hands to me,
warming my fingers that had frozen around the glass,
I was too stunned to push her away. "Oh, June! I
wish I'd known what you were thinking. I would
have set you straight, as it were, right away."

" 'As it were'? What the hell does that mean?"

She leaned back, her hands still warm and strong
around mine. "Well, let me start by telling you that
your husband is quite definitely not my type."

I was completely confused now. Her smile wasn't
helping. "What are you talking about? Tramps like
you don't give a shit about 'types' — you were just
hoping he'd give you money. And get your hands off
of me." I shoved back and Cheryl let me go.

She was shaking her head and smiling rather
sadly at me. "Money wouldn't change the fact that
he's male."

That was it. I'd had more than enough. I
struggled to get my coat out from under me and
wiggle into it without looking completely ridiculous.
"You deserve each other, you fucking bitch. I hope
the two of you rot in hell for this —"

That's when I burst into tears. I guess it was the liquor. All control was lost as I felt my face dissolve into twisted anger and shame and despair. I'd been all primed up, all ready to kill this bitch who'd destroyed my life, and then one kind word from her completely destroyed me.

"June." Suddenly she was right next to me, gently circling my shoulders with one strong arm — I hadn't realized how tall she was before — and settling my coat around my shoulders. "Come on, let's get out of here."

"My — my car — I can't —" I snuffled, the words choked and gargling out in the murmurs surging around us in the bar.

"We'll get your car later. I think we need to talk."

I was feeling so many things at once, I was so confused and disoriented, it wasn't until we were actually moving across the Bay Bridge back toward Oakland that I realized we weren't in the white pick-up.

"You don't think I meet women in bars driving that thing, do you?" Cheryl's voice still resonated with good humor, even real happiness. It made no sense. "That's just for work."

The sodium lamps on the bridge flickered in a strobe-light stream across us as we sped along. The sports car was small, sleek and black. And very fast. I watched Cheryl's hands on the steering wheel and the stick shift — the same hands that had, day after day in my backyard, held a rake or a pair of shears and grubbed in the soil. The same hands that had wiped sweat from her forehead, hitched her shorts

around her taut body, run through her hair to slick
it back from her face.

"Do you believe me, June?" she was asking. "I
would never even consider having an affair with your
husband. Or any man, for that matter."

"Oh." I squirmed, irritated with myself. Was that
the best I could do, a sort of Neanderthal grunt of
assent? And why the hell should I believe her? Or
care what she thought of me, anyway? "So, are you,
like, attached to someone?"

Again she started to giggle, made a show of
looking all around her in the car. "I don't see anyone
else here. Nope, no attachment. I'm sorry, June, I
just couldn't help it." The car swerved back and forth
as Cheryl maneuvered expertly around an immense
and aging Cadillac that quietly chuffed along the
bridge, making a good twenty miles less than the
speed limit. "Seriously, there's no significant other in
my life. I haven't had a serious girlfriend in a couple
of years."

Jesus, I was being dense. Of course, my emotional
state excused at least a fraction of my stupidity. I
raced back through my mind to try to recall my
remarks in the last twenty minutes. I couldn't come
up with anything too idiotic that had spilled from my
mouth. Except, of course, the notion that a dyke
would want to sleep with poor old Dave.

We reached the end of the bridge in silence. I
heard June draw a deep breath — suddenly I was
aware of her every movement, each small gesture and
sound coming from the driver's seat — as if she
wanted to say something.

I couldn't stand it any longer. When we took the exit for Berkeley, I burst out, "All right, I already know what you're going to say. That I'm a fool for saying all these things, for believing that —"

"Hey, hey! Calm down." We stopped at a light and Cheryl dropped her hand over mine. Again. Her fingers squeezed mine. Again. "That's not what I was going to say, June."

"Well, what then?" Now I was sounding like a cranky five-year-old kid. Even better.

The light switched and we slowly crept down the hill into Berkeley. "Maybe I shouldn't tell you this. Hell, it's none of my business." My hand still glowed where she'd touched it, and I found myself wishing for another red light. "All right. Yes, I won't deny that Dave has said — well, things to me. Things that lead me to believe he'd been looking at me."

"Can't blame him, really." Shit, did I say that? I felt Cheryl's eyes rove over me. That was a fairly neutral statement, wasn't it?

She cleared her throat. "Well. I must say, you don't seem surprised by this, June."

"About his girlfriends? His 'little flings'? I may be stupid, but I'm not certifiable yet." Her legs, caught in the glow of a streetlamp as she drove up into the hills overlooking the city, gleamed for a moment before the car plunged back into darkness. "It's just that I had to do something about it. This time, I had to stop it."

Cheryl parked the car. I saw the lights of San Francisco far below across the bay. "I thought you might like to talk a little more, June," Cheryl said softly. "This is where I live."

I turned around and could just make out, in the pale moonlight, a small white cottage nestled in beautiful old trees and shrubs. As I peered into the night, I felt strong hands stroking my neck. Without realizing what I was doing, without wanting to, I relaxed against those hands. Warmth spread from Cheryl's fingers into my neck and shoulders.

"But — I mean — I don't."

"You don't what?" Those hands were working their way across my back, kneading, massaging. "You don't watch me while I'm digging away in your backyard? You don't notice my body — the way I notice yours?"

I arched my back as she reached my waist. What the hell was wrong with me? I ought to be fighting her off, insisting that she take me back to my car. "Cheryl, this isn't what I had in mind for this evening," I managed to murmur. All of a sudden I was very warm. "Do you have the heater on or something?"

"Actually, it's what I had in mind." Now she was tracing my neck with her tongue. "I've had it in mind since you hired me."

"Really? I had no idea —" My mouth was stilled by her lips. I'm still not sure how she did it, but when we both came up for air my blouse had been unbuttoned. "How did that happen?"

"I don't know, June, but it must be uncomfortable. Here, let me help you."

So she helped me, and I let her. I let her help me with the skirt, too. All in all, she's such a helpful woman.

"Have you ever done this with someone in your

car before, Cheryl?" I asked when her hands moved to my breasts.

"Well, not right in front of my house, that's for sure." It was hard to make out her words with her mouth muffled against my throat. "I just couldn't wait any longer."

Neither could I. Her fingers traveled quickly, trailing heat and moisture over my bare skin, then landed between my legs. Landscaping work must really strengthen the upper body, I decided. That's the last clear thought I had before I came with a loud scream. Trembling, gasping, I opened my eyes and saw her smiling at me.

"Was there anything else you wanted to talk to me about, Mrs. Hammett?"

"Let me think. Perhaps —" I paused and gave in to one final shudder of pleasure — "Perhaps we could discuss it inside."

So we did. That's when I discovered her smooth skin, the firm muscles sculpted around her torso. As if it knew exactly where to go and what to do, my tongue tasted all of her, savoring every moment.

"Are you sure you've never done this before?" she asked me breathlessly.

"Never. Maybe this is beginner's luck." I moved between her legs. I wanted to hear her moan again, to feel her body writhe under my touch.

It wasn't until sunlight fought a bleary haze through the morning fog that I realized I hadn't called my husband. While Cheryl made coffee, I checked my answering machine for messages.

It was just as I figured. "Sorry, hon, Doris and I have some things to do at the office." I rolled my eyes heavenward. Sure. "I'll probably stay over in the city so I won't have to fight the morning commute. Love you, babe."

"Well?"

The cup Cheryl held out to me steamed with fragrant pungence, wiping my mind clear of the rather vulgar image of Doris, my husband's new bosomy office assistant, leaning over cleavage to drape her peroxide curls over Dave's desk.

"What do you want to do, June?" Cheryl looked away, her whole body — that delicious body — tense, anxious for my reply.

"Let's just say Dave and I are following our own paths from now on."

She looked up. "You're going to leave him?" I melted inside at the warm delight in her voice.

"Guess I'll need to start looking for a job. I'm not bad with a rake, you know?"

"Well, judging from what I've seen," she said, her arms circling my neck, "you're a pretty fast learner."

And I am. Any day now she'll promote me so I can use the weed whacker.

Looking Out on the
Morning Rain
Karin Kallmaker

I sipped my coffee and very deliberately did not think about this afternoon's deadline. I'd get another chance to do the cover photo for the *Sunday Magazine*. Sure. In about twelve years.

The problem was I lacked inspiration. The editor gave me the assignment at the top of his lungs after throwing the work of the regular photographers on the floor. "Any idiot can do better!" he had shouted, then pointed at me. "The gopher can do better. Honey, bring me a photo that won't make me want to slit my throat. In twenty-four hours." I hadn't been terribly pleased to be called an idiot, but I was not going to pass up the break that I'd been waiting for. I had glanced at the photos on the floor and boogied to my apartment for my camera bag, ready to take the cover photo for our "Winter in the City" issue.

Nearly half my time was up, and I was wasting yet more of it drinking coffee. The roll I had shot yesterday had been good work but looked suspiciously like the images on the editor's floor: black and whites of a cable car in the rain, watery sunlight glinting on Coit Tower, Alcatraz looking dark and menacing against gray waters. The light was so flat that using color film didn't lend enough contrast. All that black and gray and murky white made *me* want to slit my throat.

Why did my big break come at the same time as the worst case of winter doldrums I had ever had? There was nothing inspiring in my life. Certainly not this coffeehouse, the street outside or the endless rain.

Everyone in the place was dressed in black or gray or something in between. Even the aroma of coffee failed to move me, and I've been known to weep over a dark French roast.

I shook myself out of a daze and realized I'd been watching a woman at the counter rub the back of one calf with her other foot. For some reason she was in her socks — wet shoes, no doubt. She flexed her foot around her calf and I didn't know if it was the calf or the foot that needed the massage. The black socks padded back to a table near the window and I watched her cross her legs. Nice legs, curvy and womanly. I couldn't imagine telling the editor that a pair of black socks and a nice calf were as inspired as I could get.

The coffeehouse door opened and a burst of scratchy music accompanied a bike messenger inside. She pulled off the headphones, but didn't turn off the Walkman as she ordered her coffee. It wasn't the techno-tom-tom-Sex-Pistol-wannabe music I'd expected, but an aria — from *La Bohème*, I decided. I watched her hand rest on her belt near the Walkman. From there my gaze wandered to the black biker shorts that were partially visible through very torn and faded jeans. My gaze traced the seam of the shorts down her washboard stomach until it disappeared, just before the promised land.

Nothing ever changed. My love life never changed. I was always available for a date, and never dated. I kept meeting new women and finding in them buddies of the best sort, but buddy-bedding hadn't worked out in the past and I'd given up on the practice. So here I was, not even getting mildly bothered by a pale hand idly rubbing an abdomen of steel. Even my erotic impulses were getting bleached into gray.

My second latté was no more titillating than the first. Several more customers came and went, but nothing in their interactions was even worth noticing. I looked at my reflection in the partially fogged-up window, and saw nothing more than a blurred outline

of hair too frizzed and a leather jacket too stiff with
age. Outside the window it kept on raining. People
and bikes splashed through puddles that just refilled,
covering up any signs that anyone was going from
one place to another on this cold, bleak day.

I was almost to the bottom of the muddy cup
when I saw a flash of scarlet across the street.
Startled, I wiped at the fogged-up window with my
inadequate napkin, then the hem of my T-shirt. The
scarlet disappeared around the corner and on impulse
I grabbed my camera bag and bolted out the door.

Scarlet was moving fast. She was already halfway
down the hill. I could see the scarlet overcoat under
an umbrella emblazoned with jewel-toned toucans. A
pair of neon green sneakers tromped unswervingly
through puddles. I increased my pace to a half-run
and cursed myself for leaving my own umbrella in
the coffeeshop. Scarlet turned right at the bottom of
the hill where there was a tube to Muni. I gave up
all hope of decorum and hauled my no longer bored
butt down the hill at a dead run.

Scarlet had crossed Market with the light, which
was now against me. I kept up on my side of the
street, dodging people coming out of the tattoo parlor
and various emporiums. Scarlet had the less crowded
side of the street.

My heart was hammering and my muscles screaming for a break when I finally got an opportunity to
cross Market. I wanted to yell at Scarlet to let me
catch up, but her name wasn't Scarlet and I had no
breath to spare.

A gust of wind blew open the scarlet coat and revealed chartreuse tights disappearing into a skirt the

color of new moss. I was dying to know what kind of shirt she wore, and if it was as eye-popping as the rest of her.

One more block and I had made up half the distance. To my horror I saw her slowing to board the streetcar that was just pulling up to the island. She was the only one getting on — the car wouldn't wait for me. I sprinted and waved my arms, knowing I was making a spectacle of myself. But the driver saw me and waited the extra few seconds I needed.

I spent the next several minutes doubled over, trying to get some breath back into my body. We rumbled up the steep hill toward Diamond Heights. Just as I was recovered enough to present myself to her with some modicum of deportment, we pulled up to a stop and I saw Scarlet exit the car through the back doors. I yelped and dashed out the front doors, earning myself an angry expletive from an older woman just boarding. I said, "Sorry," over my shoulder, but she repeated it. Oh well.

Scarlet had long legs — long, slender legs with muscle and the curves I so liked. Those long legs were the only possible explanation for her being a half a block ahead again. But the sidewalk was empty and I was able finally to close the distance between us.

"Hey, hey." I gasped. "Please wait up."

Scarlet looked over her shoulder with a startled expression. She sped up for a second, then must have decided I was harmless because she stopped.

I stumbled to a halt in front of her. She looked me up and down as I caught my breath. Her lifted eyebrow made me color — I'd been so intent on catching her I hadn't thought about what I'd do when I finally did. My lack of an umbrella put me at a disadvantage; I had to peer through wet lashes to see her properly.

"I'm a photographer," I finally said. Her eyes were brilliant blue and full of amusement. Her crimson lips curved into a question and, slightly encouraged, I continued, "Can I take your picture?"

"Whatever for?" Her voice was faintly accented and I thought of gypsies. She was probably in her mid-thirties, though it was hard to tell; she could have been twenty-five or forty-five and it wouldn't have surprised me.

"The *Sunday Magazine.*"

"You're getting wet."

"It's okay." My heart was beating fast again. "My camera's waterproof and the vista behind you is okay. Can I do it?" I was so glad I'd decided to risk color film today.

"What's in it for me?"

"Uh, well. I don't know if I'm even gonna get paid." I thought fast. Her lashes briefly hid the blue eyes — the lashes weren't exactly brown or black either. I longed to see under the scarlet coat and matching cap. "Tell you what, if they use it, I'll take you to dinner wherever in the city you pick."

White teeth flashed against her crimson lips. "That's the best offer I've had in a very long time."

"Me, too," I said, before I thought better of it. I flushed again, and her laugh settled somewhere warm and south of my stomach. "Could you take off your cap and unbutton your coat?"

She arched her eyebrow again and I rolled my

eyes as if to tell her this was not a come-on. I wasn't so sure.

She unbuttoned her coat and I grinned when I saw that her shirt — which clung to her quite nicely — was electric blue. She pulled off the cap and a literal waterfall of auburn hair spilled down her shoulders and back.

I started snapping pictures. I don't think I was even breathing. Different angles, with her back to the city, with her back to the hills, with a Muni bus in the background, with her umbrella closed, with it open, with the wind whipping her coat and skirt against her body. She was alive. I was alive.

I believed that spring *would* come again.

After two rolls of color, I took one more of black and white. I had an idea for an overlay that I hoped would knock the editor's socks off.

I wanted to stay and talk to her, but time was running out. I needed to get back to the magazine's darkroom or I'd never make the deadline.

She filled out the necessary release to use the picture and I asked her to put her phone number at the bottom. As she finished the Muni streetcar heading back toward work came by and I sprinted to catch it, waving good-bye over my shoulder.

I watched her looking after me out of the back window of the streetcar. I waved, and she lifted her hand in a short salute. She looked rather bemused, but no more so than I was.

The next two hours were frantic, but the final product made me so happy I didn't care if the editor used it. There Scarlet was, in all her glorious color, against a black and white matte of the city panorama and the washed-out Muni bus. San Francisco has been compared to Oz, but next to her, it looked like Kansas.

I put the photo on the editor's desk with two minutes to spare. He was on the phone, but I had the singular pleasure of seeing him glance at the photo and do a double-take. A slow smile spread over his face.

I went to my desk and pulled out the release. Scarlet's phone number was at the bottom. I was pretty sure the editor was going to use the photo, but even if he didn't I was going to take Scarlet to dinner.

With my hand on the phone I looked at the name she'd printed on the form. "Aurora Dawn." I was grinning from ear to ear as I punched in the number. While the phone rang I looked across the sea of desks to the window.

The sun was coming out.

Coffee

Saxon Bennett

Now I can admit to myself that when I met her at the luncheon my attraction was purely sexual. She was physically beautiful, self-assured, engaging. I was three glasses of wine silly and in the mood to play. I said almost flippantly that we should go for coffee, since the members of the luncheon were dispersing. She gave me her phone number in the parking lot. I smiled and stuck it neatly in my daytimer. She was wearing a skirt with black nylons. I was entranced.

In the morning, sober and nervous I sat at my

desk and debated about calling. I twirled pencils, made paper clip sculptures, pretended to type a memo. The image of her tight ass in that black skirt and her strong hands as she balanced her plate of buffet goodies played through my mind. It was only coffee, I told myself. I picked up the phone and dialed. Her voice resonated softly across the line on the fourth ring.

"I wondered if you'd call."

"I never break a promise."

"Is that what it was?"

"I wouldn't want you to think I was playing around. I meant it. We should do coffee."

"All right. How about the Bean Hut at seven?"

"Sounds wonderful," I replied, refraining from asking what she was wearing. Her response would probably have ruined the myriad of images I had conjured up.

I slipped out of work early to wash the car, remembering the parking lot is visible from the front of the café. No sense having a nice car if I looked like a slob driving it. She was a neat woman, too neat perhaps. I could tell by the inside of her car. Everything has a place. Everything in its place. I vowed not to spill coffee in my saucer like I always do.

Rubbing the hood of the car dry I thought about her body. She wasn't a tall woman but she was well proportioned and despite her feminine office attire she seemed too fit and aggressive to be a true femme. She gave off the vibe of someone who likes to be in charge. I think of myself as independent yet I'm attracted to strong women, their dominance, their drive. Someday, I thought as I snapped the towel on the hood of the BMW, I'd like to be fucked by a woman like that on the hood of this shiny automobile.

She was already there when I arrived. Giving each other the onceover we both smiled. We were dressed almost identically, white T-shirt, blue jean shorts and Nikes.

"Obviously, we have similar tastes," I said.

"Seems like it. Here, sit. What can I get you?" she asked.

"A latté, please," I said, digging out money.

"My treat," she said.

"But I asked you out," I protested.

"You didn't break your promise. This is your reward."

I nodded. Her ass looked even better in tight shorts.

We did the perfunctories — job, sports, family. No talk of lovers. She didn't say. I didn't ask. While she responded in a well-rehearsed style, I watched her pour cream, add sugar, stir it slowly and ease the cup to her mauve lips, which left a small imprint on the side of the cup. She politely inquired the same of me. I watched her cross her legs and light a cigarette.

"You don't smoke, do you?" she asked.

"Closet smoker."

"Meaning?" she asked, smoke curling off her lower lip.

"Meaning when I'm stressed."

"Would you like one now?" she said, offering me the pack.

"Would it imply that I was stressed?"

"It could," she replied, lighting my cigarette and staring at me intently. She ran her finger around the rim of her cup. "So what is this really about?"

"Did I tell you my pet parakeet died the other day?" I replied, employing my favorite tactic of diversion. It worked every time. Women either laughed or consoled.

"You don't own a parakeet."

"I don't. Shall I get us another coffee?" I noticed we were both empty.

"Please," she said, squeezing a twenty into my hand. Her hand lingered. Her fingers were cool and long. I blushed, too addled to protest. While I waited to place my order I thought of those fingers moving quickly, firmly inside me. I felt myself growing deep crimson as I ordered another coffee black and a double latté for myself. I got the feeling tonight was going to be a long one.

She watched me from across the room as I tried to get the coffees to our table without spilling them. I felt her eyes study my body like I was a landscape she was taking in for the first time. Rolling hills, flat planes, deep crevasses, and a stretch of road to be traveled. Should I offer her a map or did she already know where she was going?

"Now that you have tarried with your response I have drawn my own conclusions," she said, taking a sip of coffee. She had applied more lipstick.

"And what might those be?"

"That this is more than coffee."

"More in what way?" I asked, spilling coffee in my saucer.

She handed me her napkin. I smiled my gratitude.
"You're nervous."

"You're making me nervous."

"Don't be. We can do this right," she said, tracing her finger along the top of my knee and watching me intently.

"Do you always speak in riddles or am I just incredibly thick this evening?"

"I'm not usually this forward but you intrigue me."

"Meaning?"

"You didn't invite me out to coffee so we could chat and then go on about our business like the casual acquaintances we are."

I confessed, "No, I didn't."

"Why did you?"

"You're not really going to make me say it?"

"I am."

"What makes you think this is more than coffee? People do go out for coffee."

"If you've kept up on the personal ads lately coffee means a cappacino or two and then fucking later."

"Do you want to be fucked later?"

"A better question, do you want to fuck me later?"

I looked at my coffee, picked up her spoon and rubbed it between my forefinger and my thumb. "I do."

"See, that wasn't so hard."

"What now?"

"Take me for a drive in that fancy car of yours."

I opened the car door for her knowing she was laying calculations on whether I would be that polite. It was a test of manners. She smiled. I passed.

She watched me as I maneuvered the car out of downtown traffic and headed for the hilltops near Lincoln. The lights would be good there.

"You have nice arms," she said, running her hand down my forearm as I shifted into fifth gear. "Firm, hard and with economy. They say a lot about you."

"You make me sound like a car ad."

"Ah, but you're so much more, aren't you?"

"What do you mean?"

"Cars, clothes and bodies say many things."

"That's a pretty materialistic attitude."

"You're not a materialist?"

"Select, perhaps."

"Because you like nice things, but not for the sake of pretention or ownership, rather for their craft and beauty."

"What are you getting at?"

"Is that how you like your women?"

I blushed. She watched me blush. She knew I would. "Yes, that's how I like my women."

"Good."

I turned onto the dirt road and stopped the car. We sat on the hood our shoulders touching.

"Good choice. I like looking at the lights. In Ohio the sky is never this clear, not like in the desert where the sky is large, unfilled, so full of possibility."

"The desert night is my favorite. It's never black and thick like it is back East. The light lingers here."

We smiled at each other.

"We have a lot in common."

"Does that frighten you?" I asked.

"No, it makes me want to know more." She ran her hand down my arm until she reached my hand, covering it with hers, then she lifted it up, sticking my fingers slowly one by one in her mouth.

I tried hard not to quiver but I did. She felt it. She wanted to make me quiver. She wanted to make me come right there. Nestling herself between my thighs, she put her arms around my neck and then she kissed me. I smelled her perfume. I tasted her lipstick. I felt her soft well-shaven legs as they rubbed against mine. I wanted to take her home.

She must have read my mind. "Take me home."

"And then what?"

"Fuck me."

"Is that what you want?"

"Is that what you want?"

"I asked you first," I said, kissing her long neck, reaching up inside her shirt to see how my hand felt against the small of her back as I drew her closer.

"I want to feel inside you."

"To see how much we have in common?"

"Yes," she said, pulling me closer.

We drove to her place. She lived in a condo uptown, tastefully decorated, appropriate prints on the wall, white leather furniture, lots of glass. It was eclectic, cosmopolitan and neat, very neat.

"Nice," I said, looking around. I stopped myself from asking if she lived alone. It was hard to tell, no photographs, no notes on the fridge, nothing to tell of how her life was lived, only well-organized sterility, like a layout in a design magazine that spoke of taste but not of the people who inhabited the space.

"Hmm . . ." She took off her shoes and snuggled up on the couch.

I sat in a chair across the room. She studied me and then walked toward me, measuring my response. She knelt down and took my shoes and socks off in slow, deliberate movements. She ran her hands up my calves and thighs, spreading them apart, kissing them, reaching her hands inside my shorts, running them around back, gently squeezing my hamstrings, ex- amining, coaxing.

I felt myself grow hot, my mouth dry. I wet my lips. "You have great legs."

"So do you."

"I wonder what the rest of you looks like." I remembered thinking how I liked women who knew what they wanted and how to get it, but I'd never known anyone like her. Anyone who could walk into my life like this, take me home and seduce me in a matter of hours. Part of me was in rapture, part was scared shitless. "Do you still want to find out?"

"I do," she said, taking my hand and pulling.

"Where are we going?"

"Where do you think we're going?"

There was a simple candelabra in her bedroom. An odd accoutrement in this house of glass and steel. She lit each thin, white candle slowly. She put her hands gently on my shoulders.

"May I?" she asked, lifting up my shirt, easing it over my head.

"I never liked this part. Clothes seem such a nuisance."

"You can make it part of the seduction, turn impediment to foreplay."

"Show me."

She undid my bra and ran her thumb around my nipple. Then she kissed my stomach, letting her tongue dive beneath the waistband of my shorts, letting them fall from my hips to the floor. She cupped her hand on my cunt, feeling the wetness soaked through my panties. She slid them down, kneeling, kissing her way up until she took me in her mouth.

I lifted her shirt off. She unclasped her bra and I felt her breasts as they rested on my thighs. They were smooth and soft and I longed for them until I lost all sense of concentration as she kissed, licked and easily slipped inside me. I ran my fingers through her dark hair, murmuring. She maneuvered me toward the bed, never removing her fingers, putting her weight on me, spreading my legs farther, filling me. I cried out and she smiled.

"Good?"

"Hmm. Come here," I said, pulling her near, wanting to run my hands down her back, her buttocks, her strong legs. She straddled me and I lifted her to my mouth, taking her in, my tongue gliding inside her. I slipped my thumb into her cunt, my forefinger in her anus looking up at her for protest. She didn't. I loved doing this, filling every orifice, giving sensation and pleasure to all the places that seek touch, that quiver with delight. She glided back and forth, crying out for more. I slid beneath her and took her from behind, reaching farther up inside her, feeling her press against me. I put my hand on hers covering her fingers. Tanned, long fingers curling around my own. Fingers missing a ring. I didn't care. She gasped and collapsed, taking me down with her.

"Oh my. Do you like that?" she asked, her eyes smiling.

"I do."

She was inside me, deep inside me.

"I feel so powerful, taking you like this," she said softly.

I couldn't answer. I could only move toward her, feeling her thighs up against mine, grinding toward her furiously. She was untiring, her long, firm, strokes even and precise. Somewhere in the distance the phone rang, ringing until the answering machine picked up and still those long even strokes, growing harder, my moving against her and wanting more. All I heard between the beep and the click was something like "I love you, darling" and "I can't wait to get home." She stopped.

"Don't stop, please don't stop."

We finished with our bodies wrapped around each other, sweat glistening across our skin in the flickering candle light.

"You're wonderful," she said.

"Ditto," I said, running my finger around her nipple.

She leaned up on her elbow and stared at me. The phone call drifted back. I could see it in her face.

I ran my hand across her lips, silencing her before she began. "I knew."

"How?"

"Tan line on the left hand."

"It doesn't bother you?"

"You're not the kind of woman to be alone."

"This can't happen again."

"I know."

The smell of coffee brings back that lingering memory. I see her dark skin next to mine, her cool fingers inside me, a single night swept up in carnal passion. Beginning with coffee ending with coffee, still spilling in my saucer. I don't drink coffee anymore. The smell, the taste of it, reminds me of her, making me crave her touch, a craving worse than caffeine or those nicotine kisses. She had let loose something dangerously primal in my veins running smooth and long like a river traveling through lost corridors in my mind. Go out for coffee? I wouldn't dare.

Slow Dance, Side of Hash
Lisa Shapiro

I'd been going to Ollie's bar after work for so long that it was hard to imagine going anywhere else. I switched allegiance because of Babs, although before the hash, it was hard to imagine Babs doing anything but tending bar. Ollie put a generous face on it when she gave notice, but everyone knew that Babs would be impossible to replace.

"Saved her tips, wouldn't you know," Torrie announced one evening, post-Babs. She glared down the bar at the rest of the regulars and demanded, "Who can save so much change?"

Torrie, offended at the notion of a savings account, peered sullenly at the beer foam sloshing in the bottom of her glass. Most of the women at Ollie's bar had regular incomes. Like the other small-town locals, we made small talk and deposits at the bank, and fretted about cash flow between trips to the post office, barber shop and fruit stand. The bar was abuzz when a woman barber moved to town. We fought over chairs in the waiting area, covering back issues of *Field and Stream* with back issues of *Hurricane Alice*. Except Ollie, of course, who fixed her own plumbing and read *Popular Mechanics*.

Ollie never bothered with an ad to replace Babs but took over tending bar herself. A week went by, not enough time for a routine without Babs. I knew Babs less than the others because of my hours at the bakery. I was often on a bar stool by two in the afternoon and, by the time Babs came on at three, I was sucking down the last of my beer and heading home. Babs' arrival at the bar had been a comfortable signal to the end of my day. Without her, I lingered, never quite sure when it was time to leave. I had stayed late again one afternoon when Torrie came around dragging rumors.

"She's opened a diner," Torrie announced. "Who would believe it?"

Torrie's general air of disbelief was nothing new, but heads along the bar nodded higher, sniffing the air for details.

"On Main Street," Torrie said. "A breakfast and

lunch place. For God's sake, Babs is going daytime."
She glared at me. "You'll probably be working the
same damn hours," she accused, as though my early
shift had somehow corrupted Babs from nightlife.

I shrugged. "Nothing wrong with working days."

Torrie slammed her glass on the bar and I hid a
smile behind my beer. I suspected that all of us had
fallen in love with Babs at some time or another. I'd
been nursing a crush with my suds for months. But
it wasn't beer that finally let me get to know Babs,
but bread.

"New account," the manager said when I walked
into work the next morning. "Bread and rolls. Take
the trays on the early run."

I made my regular deliveries first. The diner
opened for breakfast at five-thirty; I was at the
delivery door by five with an otherwise empty truck
and no need to rush. I carried the bread into the
kitchen and tried to look nonchalant when I gave
Babs the invoice to sign. She initialed it with a
flourish. I separated her copy and met her eyes.

She was a little shorter than me, although sitting
at the bar, I'd never noticed. Her dark hair, no
longer loose on her shoulders, had been braided and
wound into a tidy plait at her neck. In the daylight
of the diner her round face was scrubbed free of
worry, optimistic and eager for business.

She smiled as she recognized me. "No wonder
you're in the early crowd at Ollie's."

I nodded. "Early hours."

She sighed. "I should have switched years ago. Hours, I mean. It feels good to be up at first light."

"Will you miss the night life?" I asked, worrying about Torrie's complaints.

"I never had one. Working nights is not the same as being out at night."

"They miss you," I admitted, "over at Ollie's."

Babs laughed. "I'm three blocks down and they think I've died. I keep different hours is all. And the food is better here. No beer nuts."

"All the same," I said.

She shook her head. "It's not the same at all."

I didn't know what else to say so I clipped the delivery slip to my board and muttered, "I'll be back tomorrow."

"Wait a minute." Babs looked at the wall clock. "Grab a seat at the counter."

The clock showed five-ten. I could spare five minutes. I left Babs in the kitchen and pushed through swinging doors into the diner. I sat at the counter and looked around. A row of booths divided the windows. Blinds had not yet been raised and a sign reading "Closed" still hung in the front door. The counter stretched neatly around a gleaming grill.

Babs came out of the kitchen with a plate of food. She pushed it in front of me and my mouth began to water.

"Here." She set a fork next to the plate. "It's my own recipe. Tell me what you think."

I dug in a forkful. Steam swirled over the plate. I blew on the food, then chewed. I looked up in surprise.

"It's good." I tried another forkful. "Very good." I studied the plate as I ate: beef and potatoes, well-seasoned, finely chopped. I finally realized what was wrong. "It's red."

Babs nodded proudly. "That's honest-to-goodness red flannel hash. Take that bit of news back to Ollie's."

I cleaned the plate and licked the fork. "Thanks." She said, "See you tomorrow."

The hash was a triumph. The locals swore by it. Seasonal tourists were instructed to drive out of their way for a taste. And the women at Ollie's seemed to forget that Babs had ever done anything but cook. When it comes to local legends, collective memory is forgiving.

The red, I learned, came from cayenne and cabbage. In the summer, Babs switched to garden-grown tomatoes. The color seeped into the potatoes and stained everything with flavor. At the outset, some folks thought adding veggies to hash was a tad nervy, but they held their noses and opened their mouths and came back for more. The mayor soon declared red flannel hash part of the region's native cuisine. The mayor was a cheeseburger man, no pickles, and no one had ever heard him refer to any food groups as cuisine. But, as I said, memory is short when it comes to tradition, and Babs' red flannel hash was a tradition in no time.

I began to plan my morning deliveries a little earlier, arriving at the diner with time to spare for breakfast. At the quiet counter before opening time, Babs fed me hash and we got into the habit of conversation with a cup of coffee.

"I miss the juke box," she said one morning. "The only thing about the bar I really miss is the music."

Her comment surprised me. I hadn't known Babs to ever dwell on the past.

"I was in a diner once," I offered. "They had jukes on every table. It was nostalgic."

"Seen those in a catalogue. Music is a nighttime thing." She gestured to the TV above the counter. "Folks want news in the morning, talk shows at break time and more news at noon."

"Not the same as music," I agreed.

Babs pushed her coffee cup aside and leaned over the counter. "Just once," she confided, "I'd like someone to drop a quarter and say, 'Hey, Babs, how about a slow dance.' " She looked at me closely and my fork rattled against my plate. She stood back, laughing at her daydreams. "That would be something. A slow dance and a side of hash."

Her strong fingers gathered loose strands of hair from her neck and tucked them into their plait. I finished my coffee and slid off the counter stool.

"See you tomorrow, Babs."

She said, "I'll be here."

It was another week before I got up the nerve, and an extra three days to decide on a tape. By then, Babs and I had gone back to our regular routine. If she had any other early morning confessions to make, she didn't share them.

One morning, after I had unloaded the delivery and given Babs her carbon copy, she turned, as usual, toward the stove.

"Hold on a sec, Babs. I've got something in the truck."

She frowned at the receipt. "That's everything, isn't it?"

"Almost."

I went outside and came back with a portable tape player. I walked through the kitchen and set it on the counter. Babs followed me through the swinging doors.

"How about a dance," I croaked. I cleared my throat. "I'd like a slow dance, please, and a side of hash."

Babs turned away and walked toward the front door. I stood with my hand frozen on the tape player, my feet immobile beside the counter. She pulled the shade.

When she turned back, a slow smile danced along the edge of her lips. "What are you waiting for? Start the music."

I watched as she lifted her apron over her head, my fingers still stuck on the tape controls. She covered my hand, her fingers pressing over mine. Patsy Cline crooned through the diner.

"I thought it should be old-fashioned," I said. "Like an old diner juke box."

Babs lifted my hand and placed it on her hip. I took the hint and cupped the small of her back. She put her hands on my shoulders. I linked my fingers and pulled her a little closer. We kept on swaying gently, even when the song had ended. Then, before I could step away and stop the tape, she slid her hands across my shoulders. I felt her fingers on my scalp and my head bent to hers. And that was how I shared my first kiss with Babs — at the diner before opening time, between the day's deliveries and a slow dance.

She let go of me and smiled. "Now, how about that side of hash?"

She left the music playing and disappeared into the kitchen. I sat at the counter, listening to Patsy Cline and trying to catch my breath. I wasn't sure I could eat breakfast if I couldn't breathe.

Babs came back with two plates, which was also a new thing. Usually she just had coffee while I ate. But this time she came around the counter and sat next to me, and when the tape was through, I flipped it over and pushed the play button again.

I made it a habit after that to bring the tape player with the bakery delivery. Sometimes Babs had coffee on the other side of the counter; sometimes she sat with me and we ate together. I also came into the habit of stopping by the diner on my way home from work, which made me less of a regular at Ollie's. Instead of a beer at the bar, afternoons found me cleaning grease vents and scrubbing grills, side by side with Babs.

And sometimes, when the deliveries could wait

and the first waitress had not yet arrived on shift,
Babs would lock the delivery door and pull the front
shade. In that early half-hour of the morning, I'd
start the music and say confidently, "A slow dance,
please, and a side of hash." Then Babs would come
into my arms and we'd dance around the diner,
slowly, before breakfast.

Refuge

Tracey Richardson

Leaning heavily against her gritty pickup truck, Alex toed a dusty design on the side of her Wrangler hiking boot. Everything was caked in the fine prairie dust, even her teeth, she thought irritably, and she coughed to clear her throat.

Only her throat wouldn't clear. Just as she knew a hot bath right now couldn't cleanse her encrusted heart or rinse the stains from her soul.

With a thud, Alex let her head drop back against

the driver's side window and closed her eyes against
the hazy afternoon sun.

For a few minutes there was nothing but the
warm orange glow behind her eyelids. Then suddenly,
there she was again. First just her outline — tall,
athletic, shapely. Then, as always, her face cruelly
came into focus — the short blond hair sweeping
down to her eyebrows, big blue eyes that could look
so tender and vulnerable one minute, so hateful the
next. And there were the ubiquitous freckles and
dimpled smile that Alex supposed would forever make
Jocelyn look young, innocent.

Damn her!

Alex's eyelids burst open. Why couldn't she just
leave her alone?

Jocelyn was three hundred miles away, but her
cutting words, her unremorseful smirk, might just as
well be a breath away.

"I've met someone else, Alex."

Jocelyn's words still stung, leaving invisible welts
across her heart. It had been weeks, Alex told herself,
hoping to dull the searing, raw pain she still felt.

*Three fucking years, Jocelyn, doesn't that mean
anything to you? Three fucking years you threw away
over just one week with some bitch you met at the
conference!*

Alex was booting the truck's tire with everything
she had, imaging her silent words, the words she
hadn't been able to get out of her mouth, driving
some sense into her ex.

Finally, she leaned against the truck again, feeling
the sweat trickle down the side of her face, and lazily
hooked her thumbs through denim belt loops. It was

no use, she knew, beating herself up like this, mentally beating her lover to a pulp too. Nothing was going to change things. *Fuck her.*

Alex sighed grumpily. If only she hadn't been thinking of Jocelyn, she would have remembered to gas up the truck at the last stop. Now she was really screwed. Out in the middle of nowhere — well, Nebraska — on a seldom used highway, with all her worldly possessions and a truck that was, at the moment, useless.

Alex supposed a car would have to come by eventually. She wasn't worried — yet. She had a bottle of water, and the back seat of her Dodge Ram pickup truck had plenty of room for her to sleep. Nor did she have an agenda. She'd told her sister in Denver she'd get there when she got there, and she had enough money from her buy-out at the electric company that she was in no hurry to look for a job.

It was early evening before the distant rumble of an engine broke the quiet breeze ruffling the endless fields of corn. Alex hopped out of the truck and squinted up the highway. It was a motorcycle, a lone speck in the distance.

She stepped onto the road and began to wave both arms, heard the bike gear down as it slowed. Stopping just a couple of feet from her, the rider thankfully cut the throaty engine.

"Hey, thanks for stopping," Alex nodded to the black leather-clad figure, her own face mirrored in the black helmet's tinted full-face shield. "Nice bike," she continued, wishing the figure would speak or at least move. Her eyes admiringly combed the Harley

Davidson Heritage Softail, its chrome and leather, the tank and fenders a two-toned burgundy and cream.

A gloved hand slowly eased the shield up. Bright green eyes, large and cat-like, surveyed Alex, beginning at her feet and sliding up her stocky, denimed and T-shirted body, finally halting at her square face and brown eyes.

"Yeah," the figure nodded, patting the tank, her voice low, her accent softly southern. "It's my baby. That yours?" A thumb indicated the truck.

Alex frowned. "Yeah, but she's feeling a little neglected. I ran out of gas. I was afraid I'd be here forever."

Alex still couldn't see the woman's face clearly. Only her eyes and the bridge of her nose were visible beneath the helmet. But those eyes certainly had her attention — clear and piercing, as though nothing escaped their notice.

A leather boot kicked the chrome kickstand and the figure slid off the bike. "I can give you a lift to the next town, but my map shows it's about sixty miles away."

Alex's heart sank like a lump of lead. The biker was tall and slender, just like Jocelyn.

Alex knew there was no alternative, so she took the spare half-helmet offered her and strapped it on.

"You got a jacket or something? It gets kind of breezy."

Alex retrieved a denim jacket from her luggage and locked the cap of the truck. The bike's engine roared to life and Alex straddled the rear seat, glad for the noise of the engine and the rush of wind. It meant she didn't have to make idle conversation with this mysterious woman.

She leaned into the back rest, one hand lightly clasped around the waist of the woman in front of her. Alex smiled into the wind, enjoying the feeling of leather and power between her legs, the speed and the solitude. She even felt a little naughty for enjoying the touch of another woman's body, even if it was just leather against rough denim, the driver's narrow back slightly leaning into Alex's spread thighs.

Peering over the woman's shoulder at the empty road ahead, Alex noticed the tiny rainbow sticker on the tank's chrome gas cap and chuckled. Just her luck, to hook up with a woman who not only resembled Jocelyn, but was gay as well. Must be some kind of test, she thought, amused.

"Looks like a storm ahead," the mystery woman shouted over the noise to Alex.

Sure enough, an ominous, bruised bank of clouds loomed ahead, advancing. She felt the woman in front of her tense a little, and Alex's legs involuntarily stiffened too. Nebraska storms could be a bitch, and it was tornado season.

The Harley's engine quieted to a murmur as they turned off the highway and onto a deserted dirt road, high corn stalks waving frantically in protest of the impending storm.

"I think we should find shelter," the driver shouted. "It looks too nasty for a bike."

Alex nodded to herself and gently squeezed a fistful of leather to signal her agreement. Lightning was beginning to crackle in the distance, and getting off this hunk of metal sounded like a wonderful idea.

Rain had begun softly pelting, the wind kicking up clouds of dust, when they spotted an abandoned, weathered barn. They drove through foot-high overgrown grass and right into the doorless barn, just as the rain and hail unleashed their full fury.

With the engine cut, the booming claps of thunder more than made up for the Harley's silence.

"I'm Denise, by the way," the leathered figure said over the storm, pulling her helmet off. She shook shoulder-length hair free — hair as black and shiny as the leather it touched.

Alex had to tell herself to breathe. Her mystery biker was stunning in skin-tight leather, dark hair and tanned face contrasting so sharply with those brilliant green eyes. Her lips were full and moist, her smile dimpled. She was probably a handful of years younger than Alex.

"This storm got you so scared you can't talk?"

Alex mentally kicked herself in the ass. "Sorry, I guess it's been a rather eventful day. I'm Alex."

Denise reached for her hand and shook it, her grasp firm but warm. "Nice to meet you, Alex."

With silent curiosity and a bit of voyeuristic awe, Alex watched Denise pull her boots off, then deftly slide her leather pants down long, muscular legs, revealing dark green silk shorts.

"What a long, hot day," Denise groaned, oblivious to Alex's wide unblinking eyes. She tossed her heavy leather jacket to the dirt floor and stretched for the rafters, her dusty rose T-shirt rising tauntingly. A flat, smooth stomach peeked out.

Alex shook her head, tried to dislodge the lump in her throat. Her breath still came with a protest. She couldn't remember the last time she'd felt so quickly and so utterly physically attracted to a woman. Even Jocelyn hadn't tickled her loins that quickly.

Jocelyn.

Alex's eyes fixed gloomily on the floor. Maybe Jocelyn was the very reason for this sudden attraction. Perhaps, Alex considered, this was a revenge thing, some sort of proof that she too had it in her to turn her back on their relationship and jump into bed with someone else.

"You awlright?" A hand softly brushed Alex's cheek for an instant.

Alex flinched from the electrifying touch, felt her heart lurch and rumble like the thunder outside.

A hand took Alex's. "Hey, it's okay. I used to be scared by storms too. And these Midwest ones can be somethin' else. But we'll be awlright here, don't worry. I'm sure this barn has withstood plenty of storms in its years."

Alex's smile was limp. Hell, she wasn't afraid of storms, just of beautiful women with soothing, southern voices flooding into her shipwrecked heart. She wanted to scream out, tell Denise her whole life was one big goddamned storm right now, wanted to warn her to seek shelter. But she stood mutely, reluctant to let go of the warm hand.

"You're pretty wet," Denise suggested.

Alex froze, her jaw gaping open, and looked down expectantly, fearfully, at her crotch.

Denise convulsed in laughter, doubling over. Finally, she looked at Alex, still smiling, her eyes brimming with laughter-induced tears. "I didn't mean *that!* Though, if that's the case . . ." Her eyebrows rose mischievously, her smile widening to a grin.

Alex smiled sheepishly, her face crawling with the warmth of embarrassment, and averted her eyes. "Sorry, you must think I'm a real dork."

"Not at all, but you look pretty frazzled. It isn't just because of your truck, is it?"

Alex spread her jacket on the floor. Denise did the same beside her.

"I guess I am a little out of it these days," Alex confessed, studying her outstretched legs, feeling the cool green stare probing her, trying to mine the depths of her soul.

It was some moments before Alex dared look into those eyes, their pull finally more than she could resist. There was something hypnotic in their depths, and Alex sensed the fathomless currents stirring beneath, sucking her in. She felt defenseless, weak, like prey slowly being poisoned or suffocated by its pursuer.

"My lover of three years left me." Alex swallowed. "She just . . ." She shrugged and gritted her teeth. If she said another word, she knew she'd lose it for sure.

An arm locked around her, pulling her in. Alex roughly swatted a tear from her cheek with the back of her hand, silently admonishing herself to buck up. She cleared her throat and told Denise all about Jocelyn as fingers softly raked her short hair.

"I'm sorry," Alex said in the growing darkness, pulling herself up. "I shouldn't have laid all this stuff on you."

Denise stood too, the smell of her sun-rich skin reaching Alex. "Hey, don't be sorry. Life's too short for that shit. And look at it this way, you'll probably never see me again, so what the hell."

Alex laughed and was surprised at how good it felt.

"Look, I think we're going to be here for the night. It's getting late and this storm's not going away anytime soon. What do you say we hunker down here?"

"Sure." Alex tried to act nonchalant as she watched Denise retrieve an apple and a couple of warm cans of Budweiser from the bike's leather saddlebags. What Alex really wanted to do was get the hell away from this barn as fast as she could. She was afraid of what might happen, of what might not happen. She frowned, considering the possibilities.

"You really should get out of those wet jeans." Denise nodded.

Alex complied, draping them over the bike to dry. Her plaid Joe Boxers were damp, and she knew it wasn't just from the earlier rain.

Denise switched the bike's battery on, the headlight illuminating the barn. The rain had nearly stopped, but the wind still howled through the yawning slats. Thunder growled in the distance.

They sipped their beers, Denise stripping off bits of apple for them with her pocket knife, and they traded histories. Alex told how she took a buy-out from the power company, the breakup causing her to pull up stakes and move cross-country to her sister's in Denver. She listened, impressed, as Denise explained how she'd just graduated from the university

in her home state, West Virginia, and how years of
schooling had left her itchy to strike out on her bike
for the summer.

They talked with an ease and familiarity that in-
wardly surprised her. The storm had long ago passed;
the night was in its zenith.

"I guess we should get some sleep," Denise suggested grudgingly. After turning the bike's headlight
off, she retrieved a blanket from her kit. They lay
down on top of their jackets, sharing the worn
blanket.

"Alex?" Denise whispered. "I'm sorry you're
hurting."

Alex smiled in the darkness, feeling that, at least
for a few hours, there was someone who cared about
her. She muttered her thanks for everything Denise
had done, knowing that words somehow weren't
enough.

Sleep came quickly as they spooned together.

Dawn had begun casting gray shadows when Alex
awoke, her arm around Denise, their bodies melded
together. It was almost as though the presence of
another body, the comfort of it, the longing for more,
had overloaded her senses and awakened her. She felt
tingly wherever her body touched Denise's. Involuntarily she began caressing the long, smooth
thigh that brushed up against her own. Her strokes
were soft and rhythmic.

Denise stirred, moaning quietly from sleep or pleasure, Alex couldn't be sure. She couldn't decide if she
really wanted Denise to wake up and invite more. All

she knew was she had to touch this woman, this free spirit who had blown into Alex's life like an autumn leaf on a warm breeze. Alex knew that same breeze would carry her off again to some distant land, to someone else's barren heart. But right now she needed to feel alive again, to feel the ripening of desire.

Fingers softly guided Alex's roving hand to the silk shorts as Denise rolled onto her back, fully awake now. In the smoky light, Alex could see those dazzling green orbs searching her own, an unspoken agreement passing between them. They both smiled; they both knew what they wanted.

Alex traced the hem of Denise's shorts, then followed the groove of the inseam to their damp apex. She paused, her fingertips dancing lightly until Denise began pressing into her. Alex kissed the long, smooth arched neck, her tongue drawing wet designs there as her palm cupped Denise's gyrating mound. Soft moans escaped parted lips; Denise's eyes fluttered and clamped shut.

Alex's teasing fingers finally slipped beneath the shorts and were met with a wetness that made her smile. With her free hand, she tugged Denise's shirt up, the swell of her breasts rising with each labored breath. Alex buried her face between the tanned mounds and inhaled deeply. God, this woman was gorgeous — and the fact that she wanted Alex was just the antidote her bruised spirit needed.

Alex's mouth tackled her nipples voraciously, her fingers feasting on their own creamy dessert. The intensity of Denise's sudden spasms surprised Alex, so that she had to steady herself from being knocked off balance. She stroked Denise's face, intermittently kissing her, as the convulsions subsided.

"I want to touch you, Alex," Denise whispered, gently pushing Alex down. But she was met with a brief flash of hesitation. "It's okay," she whispered again, caressing Alex with a tenderness expected of a more familiar lover.

Alex felt her body slowly liquefy as she gave herself to Denise, the memory of Jocelyn ebbing with each pounding heartbeat. She *could* love again, and the realization made her feel as though she'd shed ten pounds of dead weight.

She was still basking in her newfound freedom when she felt Denise's mouth on her — firm, wet, gently coaxing, then more demanding. The ripples quickly swelled to rolling waves and Alex rode the crest until all at once she came crashing down in a frothy, delicious heap.

They hesitated beside the bike, Alex reluctantly handing the borrowed helmet back. It was time to say good-bye, she knew that, but she felt a tiny pang of fear. This stranger had made her realize there was life after Jocelyn, and for a few hours, there had been no sweeter place in the world. But could she find that place again, with another stranger? With someone less transient?

Denise leaned over and kissed Alex on the cheek, her eyes as embracing as her smile. "I think you're really special, Alex. I wish I could have gotten to know you better."

Alex swallowed. "You mean that?"

Denise didn't try to hide her perplexity. "Of course I mean that. Alex, you may not believe this because of what happened between us, but I don't go through women like socks or something. Last night would never have happened if I didn't care for you."

Alex grinned, her palms prickling. She took a deep breath. "You wouldn't be going to Denver by any chance, would you?"

Haunted

Penny Hayes

It's so early that George and the kids still sleep. I sit at the kitchen table, its surface cluttered with the Sunday press, Section C folded back to page three and propped against the milk carton so that I can read blabby Abby. The table sits near the window and sunshine pours into the house and warms me beneath my robe.

Steam from my half-empty cup rises, clouding my trifocals while deliciously attacking my nose. Another half-hour and one more cup and my brain should be completely engaged. I may even be able to think about what's going on in the world around me. Meanwhile, I stare at the paper, the words unreadable because my eyes have glazed over and I see, instead of print, her lovely face, haunting me, hovering before me, approximating a celestial apparition.

Haunted. Absently I nod my head, agreeing with myself as I think that that is exactly how I feel when we're not together. I long for her, painfully so, and gaze through the window at her small, white house and its green shutters just across the street from me.

It's far too early to phone. Instead, I rest my hand on the receiver which gives me a sense of connectedness to her, knowing that just at the other end of the line is the wonderful sound of her velvety voice.

I don't even know how I came to love her as I do. I suppose it grew over a period of time. We've known each other for ten years, our families having had a lot of mutual contact with our kids growing up together, and once a month, George and Scott golfing together.

After our loved ones scoot for the day, she and I usually share morning coffee or telephone to yak for a half-hour before we begin our own morning chores. One day in her kitchen as we sat across the table from each other, I found myself looking at her in a way I never had before. It scared me and for three weeks I stopped seeing her. She made no effort to learn why I cut her off cold turkey which made me so miserable toward George and the kids that they

finally threatened to disown me, not recognizing this
unusual moodiness in their caregiver.

Two weeks passed before I could no longer stay
away. It hurt me — physically hurt me — not to see
her. Giving in to my pain and after our houses had
emptied out for the day, leaving each of us alone, I
walked into her house unannounced as I'd done a
thousand times previously. It wouldn't hurt just to
have coffee, for God's sake.

She must have seen me coming because she was
waiting at the door when I got there. She remained
unmoving, silent, her chest deeply rising and falling
beneath a low-cut, light cotton print dress. I love the
way she wears those tight sundresses, causing her
breasts to press together, creating that disarming
cleavage. How had I not noticed before?

I'm jolted from my reflections as I hear George
coughing in his sleep. He's a heavy smoker and his
hacking is frequent and terrifying. The abrasive
sound shocks me and I jump, deeply resenting his
unconscious intrusion as I'm catapulted back to my
kitchen and to the paper before me.

I refill my cup before settling down again and
attempting to concentrate on Abby's advice. It's no
good. What she says is irrelevant. What my mind
conjures up, as I drift off again, isn't.

There are some first-time experiences that have to
be the most traumatizing, dynamic, mind-blowing
events in a person's life if she never sees them
coming. Somewhat like getting hit by a Mack truck.
That's how kissing her struck me as she stepped
forward, took me in her arms and pressed her mouth
hard against mine. That was when I also learned

why she hadn't contacted me while I had been scrupulously avoiding her. She had been hit by the same truck.

Perhaps if I'd kissed a woman before, this first experience wouldn't have been so powerful, so all consuming. I swabbed the entire contents of her mouth with my tongue before, gasping like a teenager, I could bring myself to break contact with her. At fifty-seven years of age, I would have thought that even with kissing a woman, I'd have been more cool, more suave. Hey, it was just a kiss, wasn't it?

"Come with me," she said. Her voice sounded like snowflakes, like down from a duckling, like a kitten seductively purring.

Helplessly, I followed her to her bedroom, stopping at the doorway. She moved to the bed and slipped out of her dress, dropping it in a flowered heap to the floor. Beneath it she wore black underwear. I never cared for black as a color for undergarments. Somehow I always thought it distasteful. But on her, snug against her smooth skin, against her all-body tan from her private backyard and long warm sunny days, against her muscular body from her frequent health club workouts, black underwear on her was absolutely dazzling.

While I stood there with my hand on the door jamb to keep myself upright while mesmerized by her to the point of debility, she reached around and unhooked her bra. She did it slowly, her hazel eyes never leaving mine. The bra was tossed aside, freeing her breasts of their bonds.

I smile, sipping my coffee, remembering. Her breasts are lovely, absolutely lovely. They sag a bit.

But they've earned it after nursing four kids and hanging around for the past forty years. Still, they are exquisite, soft to my touch, hungry for my lips if the erection of her nipples is any indication. Hard, upright, waiting. That's what they were on Monday. I smile dreamily again. And on Tuesday, and Wednesday.

Janie, my seventeen-year-old, claims she's a lesbian. She is or she isn't and time will sort it out for her. Meanwhile, here sits her old mom, dumb with love as my neighbor enters and exits my mind without as much as a by-your-leave.

I'm haunted by the memory of the extremely light brown line that travels from her navel to her pubic hair. I never saw that on a woman before. I love it because it gives me a path to follow, a place to draw my finger up and down, a guide for my tongue. I have experienced exquisite joy because of that gentle brown line. Dwelling upon it sets me to squirming in my seat.

Right now I wish my fingers were again entangled in her hair. At her age, she hasn't a gray hair on her head. I find that exotic in itself.

She says she loves my hair, too. It's white as snow, short and curly. George calls me Butch whenever I get it cut so short. He says I look like a tomboy. I am tiny and wiry, thin and very athletic, so I would have to agree with him. When I told her George's reaction, she said, "Never, ever think you're less a woman because of a short haircut. I love short hair." She buried her face against the top of my head, speaking in a very soft whisper. "You smell good, too."

I set aside the cup and ignore the paper. Closing my eyes, I relive that first encounter with her. She slowly disrobed me and took me by the hand. I remember feeling perfectly safe and secure, acquiescent as we lay down side by side. I mentally relive putting my hand upon her shoulder, and then her breast and her belly.

"Mornin', Mom." I shriek and leap wildly as Janie leans over and gives me a peck on the cheek. "Can I have the comics?"

I set aside my thoughts for the day, wipe the stupid grin off my face before I'm questioned about it, and hand her the paper.

Tomorrow's Monday.

Anna's Largo
Jackie Calhoun

My mother's lifelong friend, Elizabeth, introduced me to Anna one Friday night.

I lived with Elizabeth in a rear upper on North 29th Street, having moved to Milwaukee in the early fall from the small town where I grew up. It was nearing the end of November when I climbed the enclosed outer stairway with its dim light and found Anna sitting at the kitchen table with Elizabeth. Cigarette smoke hung in a heavy cloud over their heads.

"Anna Gagnon," Elizabeth said, "Helen's daughter, Jeanne Miller."

I stood just inside the door, suddenly shy. Anna's thick, dark hair, laced with gray, gleamed under the clouded, overhead fixture. I wondered how she managed to pull it back into a bun without a strand escaping.

Her huge, nearly black eyes crinkled at the corners as she smiled. She wore slacks and a sweater. My father would have said she was built like a brick shithouse, which somehow translated into being stacked. I'd have given a few years of my youth for breasts like hers and tore my gaze from them with difficulty.

"She looks like Helen did when I last saw her, fresh and young," Anna said, which flustered me.

I mumbled, "Nice to meet you too," while Elizabeth beamed and lit another cigarette from the burning stub she'd been smoking.

Anna shook out a Viceroy and offered the pack to me. As I took one, she pulled a Zippo out of her pocket, snapped it open and held the tiny flame toward me.

"Thanks." I drew deeply and exhaled toward the ceiling. No one had stressed the hazards of smoking yet.

"Sit down." She patted the chair next to her as if she lived here instead of Elizabeth and me. "I hear you go to U.W.M."

I shot a look at Elizabeth, who smiled and nodded, whatever that meant. I took night classes at the University of Wisconsin- Milwaukee.

"And you?" I inquired politely, still standing.

"I paint," she said, and I thought of walls and houses.

"Anna's an artist who also teaches art," Elizabeth, who took art classes herself, explained. "We've been friends since before you were born."

"Really? How nice. I'm going to change clothes," I said, escaping to my room where I could hear them talking through the thin walls. The upstairs neighbors often complained that our radio was too loud. The classical music Elizabeth loved went from mezzo piano to forte to fortissimo without warning. When the neighbors pounded on the walls, we raced to turn down the volume.

"Well, what do you think?" Elizabeth asked in a low voice.

"Lovely. Will she do it?" Anna said.

"She could use the money."

My heart began a staccato beat against my ribs. For some reason their talk terrified me. When I returned to the kitchen, Elizabeth was putting together a casserole with peas and tuna, one of her favorites. An open bottle of red wine stood on the table.

Anna poured me a glass. As I lifted it to drink, Elizabeth laid a hand on my arm.

"Wait. Anna has a question to ask you."

Looking into those dark eyes, I felt fear. "What is it?"

"I need a model for one of my classes. Would you be interested? It pays fifteen dollars a session, which lasts around an hour and a half."

"Can I keep my clothes on?" The thought of exposing myself to this woman brought color to my face.

She sighed and looked at Elizabeth, who said, "It's a professional job. Models are respected by art students and teachers. They're necessary."

Fifteen dollars was a lot of money. I asked Anna, "Do you have to know right now?"

She cleared her throat. "I'll tell you what. Come to my studio tomorrow and pose fully dressed. See how you like it."

I awoke with a thick head and stuffed nose the next day, remembering little about last night's conversation. Elizabeth and Anna had talked of their earlier years. With a start I realized I had to get out of bed and catch the bus to Anna's studio. Elizabeth had promised to go with me.

Snow was falling as we walked the few blocks to North 27th Street. The bus's air brakes released as the doors hissed open and we stepped into the damp interior. Steam rose off the wet floor and the passengers' coats. We slid onto a bench seat.

Anna's studio was on the near northeast side, a few blocks from the lake. It was one big room on the top floor of an old house with a kitchen in one corner and a screened-in bedroom in another. Her windows, ungraced by blinds or curtains, faced every direction but north. Despite the gray day, light poured through the glass panes. The wood floors were bare, and the bathroom boasted the only interior door.

Students of all ages sat on upright, folding chairs,

their easels in front of them, arranged in a semi-circle around a raised platform. All those unfamiliar faces turned toward me and I froze in terror.

Before I could bolt, Anna threaded her way through the chairs and took my arm. I heard her introduction through a ringing in my ears. She led me to the dais, while the students followed me with their eyes.

The session went well. I sat or stood as told. In fact, I quickly became bored. Fixing my gaze on a painting, an abstract with bright colors, I tried to figure it out. Just when I thought I could be still no longer, Anna told the students to put away their stuff.

Afterwards, she served Elizabeth and me coffee and sweet rolls. Always hungry, I wolfed down what they didn't eat and then walked around the room, looking out the windows. Snow was still falling, melting as it hit the pavement.

"Will you model again next week?" Anna asked as she handed me a five and a ten.

"Can I keep my clothes on?"

"The body is both functional and beautiful," she said.

"No way," I replied.

"It pays more when you pose in the nude," she countered with a slight smile and raised eyebrows.

"How much more?" I narrowed my eyes.

"Twenty."

"I can't."

* * * * *

Anna called on Thursday while I was in class and asked Elizabeth if I could come for dinner Friday night. Elizabeth told her I had no other plans, but that she did. Left without an excuse, I felt I had to go.

When Anna opened her door to me Friday night, she wore a satiny low-cut blouse and billowy pants of the same material. I looked around for a man, but there was no one else in the place.

"Are you expecting someone?" I asked as she closed the door behind me. Music from the same classical station Elizabeth listened to filled the room. She turned down the volume.

"No. Just you and me."

"Oh," I said uneasily. What would we talk about?

"Have a glass of wine," she urged, leading me to a sofa. The lamps on two end tables provided light. A coffee table held snacks, things like stuffed mushrooms. The room looked different without the chairs and easels. I asked where they were.

"Folded up behind the screen," she said, pulling her feet onto the couch under her and lighting a cigarette. She wore no shoes. It was warm in the flat.

"Oh," I said again, noticing the double bed which was now in plain view. I popped a cocktail shrimp into my mouth. The wine slid down my throat to warm my stomach. I also lit up.

"Did anyone ever tell you you're pretty?" she asked, casually curling my hair around her fingers.

My scalp tingled, and a flush climbed my neck. Even my eyes grew hot. "My mother and father." I could think of no one else.

She placed a hand on my leg, and I jumped. It didn't faze her. With a smile she walked her fingers lightly along my thigh, the muscles twitching under their passing. I couldn't figure this out. Was I stupid or what? Why was she so interested in me?

"I'm sorry Elizabeth couldn't come tonight," I said, trying to be cool and reaching for another shrimp.

"Try the mussels," she suggested, removing her hand and putting one on a cracker for me.

So that's what those were. "Thanks," I said, washing the offering down with wine. She was looking at me strangely. "What is it?" I asked, disconcerted.

"You are very young," she replied.

I bristled and said indignantly, "I'm twenty-one."

She laughed out loud. "Sorry, but that's not very old."

No, not compared to you, I thought unkindly. Elizabeth was in her mid-forties. I assumed they were around the same age.

"Are you ready for dinner?" she asked.

"Sure," I said, although I was enjoying the hors d'oeuvres. I helped her clear them away. The kitchen area overlooked the corner, and I watched a bus stop and discharge someone under the street light.

"Do you ever wonder about the other people out there?" I asked. "Where they live, what they do?" Then I flushed; she would think me stupid.

"I did when I was your age." She removed a pan of chicken in some kind of gravy from the oven. "Now I know that most lead pretty boring lives."

"Not all of them, though," I protested. In those

days I expected someone fascinating to enter my life momentarily.

"Oh no. There are always exceptions." She smiled, and it occurred to me that she and Elizabeth were among the exceptional people. "I hope you like things hot. The chicken is marinated in chipotle chili sauce. I'm part Mexican."

"Sounds good," I lied, remembering Elizabeth's admonishing me about my conservative food tastes. She'd advised, "Be a little adventurous." Now I had no choice, short of being rude.

The chicken set me on fire. I gulped water after each bite, drank three glasses of wine and filled up on the rice and beans.

She ate slowly and looked amused. "I should have fixed hamburgers and french fries."

My favorite meal, but I repeated something Elizabeth had once said. "This is an eating experience."

She laughed. "I can tell."

After dinner we stacked the dishes in the sink. She wouldn't let me help her wash them. "I'll do it in the morning."

Returning to the couch for coffee and dessert and a couple of cigarettes, I realized that she made an event out of dining.

Unused to wine, it had left me lightheaded. Since I'd turned eighteen, I'd been drinking beer, preferably Hamms. I would have died before I told her that, though.

"Do you know what I'd like to do?" she asked,

carrying our empty dessert plates and coffee cups to
the sink.

"No." I thought maybe she'd suggest a walk. "Tell
me."

Her eyes were laughing. "Lie down and talk."

"What?" It came out a half-croak, but I was too
alarmed to be embarrassed. My insides had turned
liquid. I was sure my legs wouldn't support me.

Her smile broadened, and I noticed how generous
her mouth was. "Come. Lie with me. Digest." She
took my hand and led me to the bed.

Women didn't do this, not the women I knew. I
followed mutely in her wake. I must have looked as
stunned as I felt.

"You don't have to take your clothes off." She
laughed as if she'd said something very funny.

A flush, beginning at my toes, climbed relentlessly
to the roots of my hair. I was thankful that this
corner of the room was relatively dark. Removing my
shoes, I sank into the softness of the bed and found
myself staring at the shadows on the ceiling, intently
aware of Anna's every move. Trying to relax, I began
listening to the music.

Anna shifted her weight to one elbow so that she
could look at me. I knew she was up to something,
but this was the late fifties. Although restless and
searching and lonely, I had no idea what was missing
from my life.

She leaned over me, her face in shadow. As if a
light bulb turned on in my head, I knew, and the
knowledge turned my heart into a wild thing. It

galloped around my chest, using up my breath. Her mouth was warm, soft. I'd kissed a few young men and never experienced runaway reflexes like this. Pinned to the bed by the weight of her breasts, I struggled to calm myself.

When she touched me where only a few boys had, the contrast again leaped out at me. Maybe the excitement I'd never before felt came from her knowing what she was doing. Her hand slid into my shirt and under my bra, cupping my breast that didn't quite fill it.

She leaned back, her face still shadowed. "Are you all right?"

"I can't breathe." I tried to rise, but she was unbuttoning my shirt. "Don't," I protested weakly, desire flooding me.

From the radio I heard a woman's operatic voice rising in crescendo, then descending — slow, haunting and exquisite enough to bring tears. "What is it she's singing?"

"The largo from Handel's *Xerxes*," she said. "Lovely, isn't it?"

She removed my shirt, my bra, my pants and panties with an expertise that confounded me. Before taking off her own clothes, she helped me slide under the blanket.

Her skin glowed a golden brown. Not without confusion, I watched her undress, saw her full breasts, her large nipples, her rounded belly, the black, curly mound between her legs tinged with gray. Where I was lean and underdeveloped, she was womanly.

When she reached between my legs, I lifted my hips toward her. I had never been touched intimately by anyone who knew how to excite me. Her fingers moved in long, slow strokes that quickly brought me to the edge of orgasm.

She took my hand and placed it in the wet tangle of her crotch, then moved her hips undulantly against it.

When I began to come, she slipped her fingers inside me, stopping the rush toward climax.

"Slowly," she said. "This is my largo."

Hesitantly and with a sort of wonder that I was doing this, I caressed the firm, smooth texture of her breasts. She tasted mine, and then I felt her mouth where her hand had been, her fingers slipping inside, her tongue moving over the delicate skin. I lost control, coming quickly.

"My turn now," she said, her voice hoarse.

I tasted her as she came, felt the power of her passion and my own.

After, we lay side by side, sharing a cigarette.

"Will you take your clothes off tomorrow?" she asked.

"Maybe," I said, wondering if that was what this had been about. But I felt only gratitude. By making love to me, she had made me comfortable with my body. "I'll help with the dishes anyway."

"You better call Elizabeth if you're not going home tonight," she said, bringing me back to reality.

"What will she say?" I asked.

"Whatever it is, she'll say it to me."

* * * * *

Six months later Anna gently told me to find someone nearer my age. Years after, I bought a Baroque CD because Handel's largo from *Xerxes* was one of the musical excerpts. Marilyn Horne was the artist, but to me it was and always will be Anna's largo.

So There
Linda Hill

Do you want another cup of coffee?"

The snow had started falling. Big, thick flakes silently found their way to the ground before vanishing, becoming one with the pavement. A short life.

"Claire?"

I twisted around, looking out the window in an effort to pick out a flake at the very moment it came into view.

"Hello? Earth to Claire."

I could feel a frown beginning, weighing down the corners of my mouth. I couldn't remember the sky ever looking so gray.

"Claire! Coffee!" Michael's voice finally reached my ears, and I turned back to find his green eyes squinting with disapproval. He dangled a stainless steel coffee carafe in midair above my mug.

I managed a small smile and a shrug of apology. "Yes, please. Sorry. I was watching the snow."

He snorted a reply as he poured the steaming liquid. "Daydreaming about *her* more likely."

I didn't bother denying it.

He filled his own cup before dramatically dropping himself down in the booth across from me. "This place is dead." His fingers began a quick tap dance on the Formica tabletop.

"It's nice and quiet. Enjoy it while you can." This was the beginning of the same conversation we'd had nearly every day of every winter for the past eight years. The absurdity of it struck me as funny and I had to smile, in spite of my mood.

There was nothing more peaceful than a winter morning in Provincetown. Quiet. Serene. It was my favorite time of year. Well, at least it had been in the past. But this year was different from the others. This winter felt stark. Cold. Lonely.

Before Michael could launch into his usual ramblings of "I'm going to sell this place and get the fuck off of Cape Cod," the familiar jingle of the bell above the front door announced the entrance of a lesbian couple, cheeks bright red from the cold, frosty air.

"Customers," Michael trilled under his breath

before jumping up to greet them and usher them to the best table in the place. I had to laugh again, knowing that the same couple would never receive such a greeting in the middle of July.

Michael's restaurant was a cozy little spot near the east end of Commercial Street. While the restaurant was known for its exquisite seafood cuisine, its real draw was that it served the most incredibly luscious breakfasts on all of the Cape. You counted your lucky stars if you found an empty table before noon during the summer season.

Michael and one of his lovers/business partners had opened the place nearly twelve years ago. There had been so many lovers since then that no one could actually remember which one had been the original partner. But he'd begun to settle down over the past few years and it was David, his lover of three years, who was currently in the back dreaming up new exotic breakfast dishes to trot out next spring.

A gust of cold air brought chills to the back of my neck as the jingle sounded again.

"Claire!" I recognized Charlie's voice before he reached my table. He was out of breath, cheeks pink behind a full beard. "Are you opening today?"

"Why?" I sent him a lazy smile. "You wanna buy a book?" I owned the small women's bookstore next to Michael's. Not *the* women's bookstore. Just a small little bookstore/coffeehouse that catered to the throngs of lesbians that poured down Commercial Street every summer.

"Very funny," he grimaced, unzipping his down jacket. "I need a favor. I have to run up to Boston to pick up a part for the Jeep and I have two incoming."

Charlie ran the town's only limousine service. He spent most of his time during the busy season driving back and forth to the small airfield out by Race Point Beach. *Two incoming* meant that there were two passengers flying in from Boston that day that needed to be picked up and brought in to town. Charlie often asked me to fill in for him.

I narrowed my eyes. "A couple?"

He nodded. "Dykes. Ever notice how they only come in pairs during the off-season?"

I sighed and waved him away, ignoring his sarcasm. "No problem, Chuck. Where are the keys?"

"In the limo." He grinned, already edging toward the door. "They're on the one o'clock. Don't be late."

Don't be late. Of the fifty or so times I'd helped Charlie out, I'd been late exactly once. That one single time back in June, when I'd left a group of seven stranded for nearly an hour before remembering that I'd agreed to pick them up. But it had been the first beautifully hot day of the year, and I'd gotten caught up out back of the store, soaking up the sun and enjoying the scenery of baby dykes strolling up and down the coast.

I ended up dashing to the airport, dressed in a T-shirt and shorts, screeching to a halt outside the landing strip and smiling apologetically at the scowling faces. Well, six scowling faces. And one crooked smile that went with an equally crooked raised eyebrow. She'd hung back a little as I ushered the others into the back of the limo and stowed away their luggage.

"Hectic day?" she asked as I shut the door behind the other passengers. I looked her up and down, appreciating her smile and the dark hair that framed her face. A single diamond studded one nostril, and a pair of dark, trendy sunglasses hid the color of her eyes.

I decided to tell the truth. "Daydreaming."

Her smile widened to reveal perfect white teeth, and she laughed. "At least you're honest."

"Most of the time," I quipped, deciding that I liked her. I extended my right hand. "I'm Claire Mathews."

The hand that met mine was much smaller than my own. "Toni Westfield. Nice to meet you."

My jaw dropped. "Toni Westfield? The author?" I thought I saw her blush as she nodded.

"Most people don't usually recognize the name." She wrinkled her nose.

"I own a bookstore," I explained. "I've read all your novels."

"A bookstore? That's cool. Which one?" It was Toni that motioned toward the car, reminding me that I had four men and two women in the limo who had already waited over an hour.

"Oops." I laughed guiltily and ran to the driver's side of the car. Toni slid in to the passenger's seat and we drove quickly in to town.

During the brief drive, I learned that Toni had decided to come to Provincetown for the summer to finish writing a novel that was already a month late to her publisher. She explained that she and her lover of four years were having some troubles, and they had agreed that Toni should take the time to focus on meeting her extended deadline.

Since moving to the Cape and opening the bookstore nearly eight years ago, I will admit to having had a few small crushes and even a few brief affairs. But my general rule of thumb was that I didn't get involved with anyone who would be in town longer than a week. A weekend was even better. The locals all agreed that the real recipe for a broken heart in a seasonal place like Provincetown was becoming emotionally attached to someone who would be around for the entire summer. Particularly someone as young, successful and charming as Toni Westfield.

I broke my own rule. We even had dinner the very night she arrived. And nearly every night after. She worked alongside me in the store, graciously signing autographs and bashfully fielding the most flattering advances from anyone who recognized her.

Our days became a steady diet of sunshine, ocean, books, sunsets and intense conversation. While she always carried a writing tablet and pen, I rarely saw her write down a single word. This frustrated her, I knew. But when I tried ask how the novel was going, it only seemed to cause her greater frustration.

"You know how it's going," she whispered late on the fourth of July. "It's not. So there."

"Anything I can do?" I'd asked.

"Cease to exist," was her quick retort, and for the

first time that evening I witnessed a moodiness that
I knew I was partly responsible for. "I don't mean
that," she told me.

"I know."

"I came here so I could focus and write, and all
I've done is moon over you."

I'd laughed at this. Toni didn't moon. She in-
vested.

She hesitated a moment before making a con-
fession. "You know I lie in my bed every night and
think about what it would be like making love with
you."

I smiled, knowing I'd done the same.

"I want to. So much."

"I know. Me too."

"But we can't. There's Brenda . . ." Her voice had
trailed off as she said her lover's name. So while I
hated the fact that the line had been drawn, I also
respected her for it. I never pushed. As often as we
held each other. As much as I wanted to. We never
made love. And I never heard her mention Brenda's
name again. Not until Labor Day weekend. Exactly
one week before she was scheduled to leave.

We were in the back room of the store. I was
sitting at my desk while she sat in the over-stuffed
chair, pen and paper in hand.

"What?" She looked up at me, blinking hard.

"I was just wishing that you could see P'town in
the winter. It's gorgeous. It's quiet. Snow is piled
everywhere." I couldn't help the slow smile.
"Romantic."

"Romantic?" Her eyelids dropped a fraction as she said the word. "I wish I could see it. I've never seen snow before."

"What?" I didn't believe her for a minute.

"I've never seen snow," she repeated, then dropped the ballpoint pen to her lap. "Honest."

I stared at her, still not believing. "How can you be alive for thirty years and never see snow?"

"By living in Brownsville, Texas, all your life," she chided me. "It never snows in Brownsville." She stood up, both pen and paper falling to the floor, forgotten as she approached and knelt down in front of me. "And I have not yet lived thirty years. So there." She punctuated the last two words with a pointed finger to my knee.

"Twenty-eight is a whole lot closer to thirty than to twenty," I reminded her. "So there." She was leaning so close that I could see the tiny dark flecks of her blue eyes.

She was grinning, enjoying the teasing as much as I was. "And by that logic, I guess we could say thirty-seven is a whole lot closer to forty than to thirty." She laughed.

"Ouch." I grimaced.

"So there." She stuck out her tongue and I suddenly had an image of what she must have looked like as a child.

My eyes narrowed. "You were a spoiled brat when you were a kid, weren't you."

Her smile faded. "Brenda says I'm still a brat."

The mood that had surrounded us evaporated the instant she mentioned her lover's name and we were reminded of how short our time was. She would be leaving soon. Returning to Brenda.

I reached out to brush a stray curl behind her ear. "Are you?" I asked quietly.

The corners of her mouth turned down briefly as she pouted. "Maybe." She smiled shyly. "Sometimes."

I chuckled softly, knowing it to be true. Her gaze met mine and I felt my heart becoming too big for my chest and had to sigh, force the air from my lungs to make room for the swelling of my heart.

"I am going to miss you so much." The words were out before I could stop them, hanging in the air between us.

She stared at me, clearly as surprised to hear the words as I was to have said them. "I have to go back." Her voice sounded odd. Strained.

"I know." My heart imploded. "I'm sorry I said that. I didn't mean to."

"I have to be fair to her."

What about being fair to me? I wanted to ask.

"I have to give her a chance."

What about giving us a chance? I was raising my hands, trying to silence her without words. I didn't want to hear any more about Brenda.

"Claire." She was reaching out for my hands. "We've talked about all this."

"I know. I know." But knowing that she'd be leaving from the moment we'd met didn't change the way I felt now that it was nearly time. It didn't stop me from wanting her to stay.

"Claire."

"Please." I tried without success to pull my hands

from hers. "I'm sorry I said it. Please. Let's drop it, okay?"

The silence between us grew uncomfortable. I watched as anger and frustration rose on her cheeks. "You don't get it," she began tersely. "You think it's *you* that I'm leaving. But it's not like that. I made commitments. To Brenda. To my publisher." She leapt to her feet and began prowling the room. *"Christ.* I came here to finish that fucking book and I've barely written one chapter in two months." She ran her hand through her hair and I watched her struggle, cursing myself for saying those words. "And why haven't I?" She stopped before me, the fire in her eyes quelling as her voice softened. "Because I want to spend every possible minute with you."

I felt my heart swelling again.

"You think I won't miss you," she said quietly. "But I will. I think about little else."

I reached out a hand and she took it, squeezing it gently.

"Really?" I asked, stupidly.

"Really, Claire. I love you." She said the words simply, her gaze holding mine as a mischievous glint crept into her eyes. "So there." Her tongue made another brief appearance and I laughed, tugging her down to my lap. "So there," she whispered again, just as her lips found mine.

We fell asleep in each other's arms every night that week. On her last day in P'town, I drove her to the airport in silence, holding her hand and trying not to break down.

When it came time for her to climb the steps to the plane, we held each other tightly, both sniffing and brushing back tears that wouldn't stop. She blew her nose and cursed the diamond stud that adorned her nostril.

"I always wanted to ask you why you pierced such a lovely nose," I tried to laugh.

"I don't remember. But it was the cool thing to do at the time, though." She sniffed.

Our gazes locked and I searched her eyes, trying to commit every line of her face to memory. "You'll outgrow it," I declared.

She considered this for only a moment, then nodded. "Probably."

I wasn't sure if we were talking about the nose ring or about us. I felt myself begin to crumble.

"But I won't outgrow you, Claire Mathews." She kissed my lips soundly and began backing away toward the plane. "I'll be back. I promise." She nearly ran up the steps, pausing just before stepping inside the plane. "So there," she yelled, and waved.

"So there," I yelled back, and I watched the plane take off and fly her right out of my life.

I thought about her now as I slid behind the wheel of the limo and began the trek out to the airfield. I told myself that it was time to let go, as I did many times each day since she'd left. Then I cursed myself as I neared the airport and saw that the little Piper had already landed.

Unlike the last time I'd been late, the couple that waited were happy to see me and chatted up a storm as they slid into the car. I tossed their baggage into the trunk and slammed it shut just as the familiar voice reached my ears.

"So this is what snow looks like." There she

stood, overdressed in a hooded parka and boots nearly as high as her knees.

Stunned, I covered the distance between us in a few easy steps. My eyes raked her features, taking in every detail. "What happened to the diamond?" The nose ring was missing.

Her grin was lopsided as she shrugged. "Guess I outgrew it."

I laughed, for the first time in months, and felt it deep in my belly. My hands found their way to her shoulders. "How's the novel?" I asked.

"Finished," she answered.

"Congratulations. And Brenda?"

"Finished," she repeated.

I nodded quietly. "Are you really here?"

She nodded, gloved hands sliding up my forearms. "You didn't believe I'd come back, did you."

I shook my head, the shock of her arrival almost wearing off. Our arms slid around each other, awkwardly at first, then strengthened.

I kissed the tip of her nose. "So I was right about the nose ring."

"Yes, Claire. You were." She sighed playfully. "And I told you I'd be back," she whispered against my ear.

"Yes, sweetie. You did," I admitted.

She lifted her head, and I could see the mischief in her eyes. "So there," she told me, laughing that impish laugh.

"So there," I replied, catching her tongue gently between my lips and kissing her.

Between the Seats
Kaye Davis

When Doni pulled the trigger on the ignition timing light, the strobe flashed on the crankshaft pulley mark and the scale. Perfect, Doni thought. The rebuilt four-hundred-cubic-inch Ford engine, with three hundred break-in miles on it, was within spec after a little fine tuning. Reaching into the open door of the 1978 red and white Bronco, she cut the engine.

"Sounds great," Jeb said, tightening the last screw

on the sun visor. "Interior is finished. When are you going to show it to Carol?"

"I don't know. I'm not sure she wants to see me or the truck." Doni jerked off her black cap and wiped her brow with a shop rag. It was a hot May afternoon and the cap was damp with sweat. She noticed with irritation the grease stain that blemished the silver State of Texas seal and streaked across the bold print that read *Assistant Commander, North Texas Narcotics Task Force*. She disconnected the timing light and put away her tools.

"You're all she talks about, and she hasn't seen the truck since you finished the engine and had it painted." Putting a hand on his hip, he added, "Girl-friend, I know you love her. Do something about it. Besides, I want her to see my upholstery work."

"Your upholstery is beautiful."

"I know that. Got to run." He tossed her the screwdriver. "Call her. It's Friday — take her out. Go to a happy hour, have dinner. All you've done in weeks is work on this truck."

"It was therapy, Jeb."

"I know, Doni, but was it physical or mental?"

"Both maybe," she said, waving to him as he got into his black Maxima and drove off. Call her, he says. It sounded so simple, but what could she say? Her best apologies were much too inadequate.

She admired the gleaming engine with its chrome valve covers and air breather. Sexy red and silver liners covered the hoses and vacuum lines. The truck, almost show quality, was fast with brand new steel racing valves and a special cam. The multi-layered paint job and new blood-red interior had completed the restoration.

Pain shot up her right arm and into her shoulder when she slammed the truck hood. She thought of her pain as an evil entity that never retreated, never retired and constantly lurked in the background waiting to spring out at her. She was learning not to be surprised.

She went inside to shower. The message light on her answering machine blinked impatiently at her. It was Roy and she'd just missed the call. He said, "Wanted to tell you they got the doctor's recommendations from your last check-up and they'll make a decision soon. Don't forget Clint's birthday party tomorrow. I hope you and Carol can make it. Speaking of Carol, Becky had lunch with her Monday, but wouldn't tell me what they talked about. 'Bye."

Doni had a pretty damn good idea what they talked about. God, she'd always sworn she wouldn't make the same mistakes the male officers did. But she had. Blame the seven-year itch, that reality disguised as a myth that she didn't used to not believe in. Blame being gone too long, too often. Yet, the storm might have passed if not for the shooting. She could remember that cold Dallas night like it was yesterday. Moments before they raided the crack house, a blue norther had swept through, dropping the November temperature thirty-five degrees in an hour. Combined with the full moon, it should have been enough to warn them.

When they kicked in the door, she ran inside shouting, "Police!" No one believes her, but she

swears time slowed to a trickle. She saw the bullet
leave the barrel of the crook's Glock nine millimeter
and tracked it coming toward her until she lost it in
the flash of her own nine millimeter Colt. Her Kevlar
vest caught the first bullet, but the second bullet
struck two inches above her right elbow and
splintered into fragments after it shattered the bone.
Traveling along the humerus, one of the larger fragments embedded in her right shoulder, damaging the
joint. Her assailant wasn't so lucky. Her bullet
pierced the doper's lower throat and blew out the
back of his neck. He strangled in a geyser of his own
blood while Doni, on the floor six feet away, watched
in fascination. Roy got a tourniquet on her before she
bled to death.

After the shooting, Carol met the ambulance at
the emergency room and didn't leave the hospital for
three days. She begged her to take a medical
retirement from the state or at least to get out of
narcotics. Doni's shoot-out was the second for the
task force in two years. In the first shooting, Snake,
Doni's mentor and buddy, had been killed in a
routine buy/bust that turned into a robbery. Doni
refused to quit, and Carol didn't know if she could
stand the waiting and worrying if Doni went back.

Their strained relationship came unwound six
weeks ago when Doni met Trish, her new physical
therapist. Trish was young, enthusiastic and beautiful
with thick black hair, and she supported Doni's goal
to return to active duty. Trish's lover had left her.
Doni was restless and depressed. Their needs meshed.
Twice they went to Trish's apartment and . . . what?
Fucked? She damn sure couldn't call it making love.

And it wasn't enough. They broke it off, agreeing to remain friends. When Carol pinned her down and demanded an explanation, she couldn't lie. The next day Carol moved into an apartment.

Roy and his wife, Becky, were good friends to her and Carol. He was acting assistant commander in Doni's absence. Even Roy hadn't been immune to infidelity. He'd had a brief affair with a female snitch that caused Doni personal and professional distress. As assistant commander of the task force, Doni almost had to fire him and did suspend him for a month without pay. Luckily, he came to his senses before he lost his job, his wife and three-year-old son.

With her right arm shaking, partly from the exertion of working on the Bronco, partly from anxiety, she dialed the number for the Dallas advertising firm where Carol was the CEO's executive assistant. Although she had a degree in business management, she was taking courses in advertising and marketing at night. She already made more money than Doni and her salary would rise dramatically when she finished school.

When Carol came to the phone, Doni blurted, "Hello, want to go for a ride and maybe have a drink?" Damn it, she'd planned a smoother beginning.

After a long silence, Carol said, "It's finished."

"Yes, I thought you'd like to see it."

"I don't know, Doni."

"I want to see you, Carol. Come on — for a short ride and a drink. We need to talk."

"That's an improvement. Before, you always avoided talking about our problems. Pick me up here at six."

* * * * *

Wearing beige tailored trousers, a white shirt and a dark green vest, Doni waited in the valet circle in front of the office complex. Carol came out of the glass revolving doors wearing a gray pin-striped suit with slacks. At thirty-five, she was more beautiful than ever. Carol's amber hair, small waist, well-defined hips and full breasts ignited a dull ache in Doni. How could she have cheated on this woman, Doni thought, opening the door for Carol.

"You're letting me drive?" Carol smiled, tossing her purse between the seats. Looking Doni over in a sweeping glance, she asked, "How's the shoulder?"

"Much better. I won't need the third surgery." It only hurts when I breathe, Doni wanted to add, but she said, "You ought to see how good the engine looks."

"Well, don't show me in the valet circle." Carol turned the key. The truck jumped when the engine roared to life.

"Careful, baby, she's got a sensitive accelerator," Doni said as she leaped into the passenger seat.

"So do I, so we'll get along well." Their eyes locked momentarily and Carol said, "I've missed you, Doni." She adjusted her seat and put the truck in drive. "Sue Ellen's?"

"Carol, I want you to move back."

Not responding, Carol floored the accelerator, throwing the transmission into passing gear. The front end of the Bronco reared in response and the raw horsepower pressed them against their seats. For the first time in several weeks, Doni saw Carol laugh. She sped across the busy service road and entered Interstate 635. Slowing the truck to fit the flow of the traffic, she glanced at Doni. "Not only do I have to worry about someone shooting you, I have to worry about you killing yourself in this."

"Don't worry, I can handle this baby. Come home."

"I can't," Carol said, a slight catch in her voice as she followed the left split off 635 and blended into the southbound traffic on Interstate 35. "Life with you has too many high highs and low lows. Do you understand what I'm saying?"

Doni nodded. Her arm and shoulder throbbed. The pain was worse when she was tense. She was losing everything — Carol, the house, maybe the job. Carol could afford the house. But Doni, like every other recently divorced police officer, would have to provide security at an apartment complex in exchange for free rent.

The warm May sunset drew them to the front patio at Sue Ellen's. When they were seated with a Crown and Coke for Carol and a Michelob for Doni, Carol said, "You've got to talk to me. This is why I wanted you to go to counseling with me."

"If we're going over that same old ground again we may as well leave now."

"What are you going to do if the doctors don't clear you for active duty?"

"They will. My right arm and shoulder are getting stronger every day. Working on the Bronco helped my dexterity. If I have to, I'll learn to shoot left-handed."

"I hope you get to go back since it means so much to you. But aren't you afraid, Doni? Just a little bit?"

"During the shooting I didn't have time to be afraid. Afterwards, I hurt too bad."

"Well, I have enough fear for both of us."

"Carol, all I ever wanted was to carry a badge like my uncle and my dad. I studied everything they did and said, and I learned well. Narcotics work is all I know, and I'm good at it." Doni studied her nails. "I lied to you just now. I am afraid. I'm afraid they won't clear me to go back." Looking up, she smiled, feeling wistful. "I was going to be the next commander when Frank retires. It would have been easier for us then."

Doni saw Carol's frown melt and her dark brown eyes soften. "Maybe you can still make commander."

"Maybe." The wanting for Carol cut through Doni's chest like a Black Talon bullet through Kevlar. Part of her yearned to grab Carol's hand, drop to her knees and beg her to return, but she couldn't, wouldn't, do it. She drained her beer. Looking at Carol, she felt like she was sitting too close to a fire, but the sense of loss blistered her worse than any fire could. "I guess it's time to go," she said.

"I had lunch Monday with Becky."

"I heard."

"She thinks all of our problems started after Snake got killed."

Doni tore at the label on her empty beer bottle.

"Yesterday I had lunch with Trish."

"Why?" Doni asked, letting the irritation show in her voice.

"I'm trying to figure you out, Doni — since you won't tell me anything. I understand why you were attracted to her."

"I told you before that she is a good person. You can't blame her for what happened."

"I know that. I think there were several contributing factors. Between my work and school and your work hours, we've become strangers living in the same house."

"I think that's an exaggeration."

"I've gone over all of this with my therapist."

Great, Doni thought. She resisted the urge to roll her eyes.

"It's not just the work hours," Carol said. "When you're off, you spend most of your time with Roy and the other guys. You don't like my friends. You won't go to any of my work socials with me. I can rarely get you to participate in anything in the gay community. Doni, it's not just that your job scares me. It's the way it dominates our lives."

"What do you want me to do, Carol? Your fucking liberal friends and co-workers show no respect for me, the job or anything I believe in. The last goddamn party you drug me to they were smoking dope in the driveway and snorting coke in the bathroom. If I'd known who it was, I'd have busted their asses. Yet they're the first ones who complain when some dope fiend breaks into their Lexus or burglarizes their home." She frowned at Carol who seemed close to tears. "I don't think our life together is that bad. If you do, why'd you even agree to see me."

"Because I love you. And because it's not all bad. You're good-looking, fun and exciting. You have courage and convictions. When we're together, you treat me with respect and consideration — not all couples have that. I know you love me and you are — or were — faithful."

"That won't happen again."

"I know." She sighed. "On the other hand, I wish you were more open to me with your thoughts and feelings. As to where this leaves us, I don't know. I guess we have to decide if we're happier with or without each other."

"I know what I want. I want you to come back home."

"Maybe it is time to go." She pushed her chair back. "You did a good job on the truck. I'm impressed. Snake would have wanted to buy it back."

Doni rose and took Carol's hand. "Thank you. I never could have finished it if Roy and the guys hadn't helped put the engine back in. Jeb wants you to check out the upholstery."

They rode back to Carol's office in silence. Carol, leaning against the door, seemed lost in thought. Doni didn't disturb her. The Bronco's duel exhaust echoed loudly in the deserted parking garage when Doni stopped in the slot next to Carol's white Mitsubishi convertible. She shifted the truck into park and set the emergency brake.

She stroked Carol's hair and touched her cheek. "I'm sorry for what's happened to us."

Carol came into Doni's arms and they kissed. Doni's heart leapt with desire and hope as Carol's lips parted. Her hands couldn't stop moving. She frantically sought and released the buttons and zippers binding Carol's clothing. Reaching under her loose bra, she cupped a soft breast and found a rigid nipple. She lowered Carol to the red carpet between the front seats and pushed her bra up to expose both breasts. Sliding Carol's panties and slacks over her hips to her knees, Doni caressed her soft curly hair before slipping her fingers inside. Abruptly Carol sat upright on the floor and scooted closer to the front of the truck. Kicking one leg free, she threw it over the hump with the four-wheel-drive shifter and opened herself for Doni. She grasped Doni's wrist and pulled her fingers deeper inside her. Doni kissed her lips, her neck and breasts, but the awkward position started a burning sensation that radiated through her shoulder, upwards and downwards, numbing her cheek and deadening her hand.

She pushed into Carol and withdrew, increasing the tempo. After a few moments, Carol grabbed Doni's wrist again and drew her fingers to her clit. Soon, Carol stiffened, twisting her fists in Doni's shirt. Doni didn't remember the engine was running until Carol's leg straightened, smashing the accelerator flat.

When she came, she moaned, "Oh, my God, Doni. Oh, my God."

Doni risked a glance at the RPM gauge and prayed her three-thousand-dollar engine held together without blowing a gasket or breaking a valve spring. Carol jerked her foot off of the accelerator and frantically tugged at her clothes.

"Amazing how sex brings out the religion in us all," Doni said, amused at Carol's distress.

"I can't believe you did that to me here. What if the security guard came out? I have to work here, you know. What if we'd been overcome by carbon monoxide poisoning and found dead like this in the morning?"

"At least we practiced safe sex. We were parked and had the emergency brake on." Doni laughed, watching Carol stretch out in the passenger seat and button her slacks and blouse. Carol scowled at her, but Doni suspected she was trying to suppress a smile. "I'll tell Jeb you liked the upholstery." An invisible hot dagger plunged into her shoulder and Doni grimaced with pain.

"Are you okay?" Carol asked, lightly touching her arm.

"No, I want you to come back to the house."

"That's not good enough."

"Damn it," Doni said. Her temper flared and she slapped the steering wheel. "What do you want me to say? I can't change what I've done. It was a mistake and I'm sorry it happened. I can't give up my career." She took Carol's hand. "I need you to help me put my life back together. I'm lost without you." Her voice cracked and she struggled for composure. "I love you, and I need you. We can work out our problems. I can make some changes. We'll do what it takes to get through this. Please come back home."

"That's what I had to hear." Carol sighed. "I had

to know that you're willing to work with me. It won't be easy for us and I plan to keep my apartment for a while. It'll be hard for me when you go back to work, but I know I can't hold you back." She wiped a tear away and smiled. "In the meantime, I know how to improve your dexterity and strengthen your arm and shoulder."

Doni watched until Carol was safely behind the wheel of the convertible. Smiling, she glanced at her wristwatch. It was only nine. She wondered if it'd make Carol angry to know she'd put clean sheets on the bed before leaving to pick her up.

Carol backed out off the parking place slowly and Doni saw her talking on the phone. She slammed on the brakes when Carol stopped the car and jumped out. Doni rolled down her window.

"Congratulations," Carol said. "Roy just called looking for you. He said your vacation is almost over. In two weeks, if you can qualify with your firearm, you're back to active duty. But for the really good news — they've postponed interviews for task force commander until next month. You might still have a chance. Let's go home and celebrate."

Somehow the pain in Doni's shoulder seemed more bearable as she followed Carol home.

Teacher, Teacher
Catherine Ennis

It was shortly after she was hired that I learned there was a new "committee member" on campus. Word spreads fast in our group. She had her doctorate, was in the math department, lived alone in the hi-rise condo off campus and was deep in the closet. So, how did we know? All I can say is that it takes one to know one. I think it was their department secretary who spread the word. So, get in touch with her, my friends urged.

I was interested. My live-in had wandered off with

a nurse who worked in the ER, leaving me with her piano and the cat. I felt sealed off, boxed in, and lonely as hell. Not to mention missing sex. Our mystery woman sounded intriguing, and I was almost raw from wanting someone, but I'm too shy to make a direct, frontal approach.

She was described as tall, slender, attractive, thirtyish, smart as hell but not much of a talker. All of those things sounded fine to me. What really caught my attention was the fact that she had started jogging around the library building before class in the morning.

I ran, too, usually starting my run around the library a few minutes before seven, so I figured I'd try to meet her somewhere along the way . . . accidentally, of course. Somehow I'd make contact without being too pushy. If I could think of anything to say, that is.

I was tightening my laces when I saw her. She wasn't wearing running things, just slacks and shirt and ordinary tennis shoes. Actually, she wasn't running, just walking fast and swinging her arms. She was concentrating so hard she didn't see me swing off the library steps.

We crashed. It took a minute to untangle arms and legs. She asked, "You all right?"

"I'm okay," I said, and I smiled at her.

"Good." She didn't return my smile. With a nod so slight I wasn't sure I really saw it, she walked away from me, gaining speed. I followed at a discreet distance, then I sprinted ahead; neither of us spoke as I passed.

The next day I sat on the steps again. This time

she saw me, and she veered to the edge of the sidewalk so we wouldn't collide. "Hi," I said as I walked alongside her, taking a few seconds to match her brisk stride.

"Hi," she answered, not looking at me.

"You okay?" I sort of chuckled. "No broken bones or bruises from yesterday?"

"No." Her pace didn't change.

"Well, that's good. I wouldn't want to cripple anyone."

She took a deep breath, I saw it. I waited for her to say whatever it was she needed so much air to say but she kept walking. That's when I decided she must put words together only when she had an interest in what was going on . . . no idle chatter for her. I suspected she wasn't interested in having a conversation with me. That was okay, I had time.

We circled the building, dodging runners coming at us and parting to let others come between us. I say "walking" but she kept up a pace that was almost as good as my jogging time.

When we reached the steps at the front of the building, I stopped. She kept going. " 'Bye!" I yelled after her. I think she nodded, but from the back I couldn't be sure.

I walked alongside her for several days. I'd greet her, but she didn't say anything to me as I moved to the sidewalk and fell in step. Maybe she was monitoring her pulse or counting the cracks in the sidewalk or something. Twice around the building my time ran out and I had to quit, but she kept going. No good-bye, either. She simply moved on.

I decided it was time for me to look for greener

pastures. I was attracted to her, and by now my interest was more than casual, but I wasn't getting anyplace. I had been told that she was aloof. My thinking was that she was probably deep into a long-term relationship we didn't know about and was simply not interested. I'd try one more day. That's all.

When I took my place beside her that Monday morning, she actually turned, looked me smack in the eyes and smiled. I almost stumbled. "Well, hello," I said. "Hope we finish before the rain." The sky was black, the wind gusting, and it didn't look like we would.

"Yes," she said, "but it doesn't look promising."

"I'm Mary Ellen," I said ten steps later. It had taken me that long to compose what I wanted to say.

"Peg," she answered. "Short for Peggy."

Now that I had a name, I might as well use it. "Peg," I said, "I don't have to go in until ten o'clock tomorrow. Do you have time for breakfast after we run?" This was a long speech and certainly out of character for me, but if she wasn't interested I would just move on. We'd been "in step" for so many days I figured I wasn't being too forward. She could tell me to get lost, couldn't she?

Six steps later she said, "The cafeteria?"

"I think they serve until nine. Sure." I almost tripped over my own feet, glad we'd reached the steps so I could sit and replay my invitation and her acceptance.

"After our walk." And she kept going. I watched until she rounded the corner and was out of sight.

* * * * *

As I heated yesterday's leftovers for my supper that night, I kept remembering the little flash of something in her eyes when she smiled at me. Amusement, maybe? Like she'd been expecting me to say just what I did. Whatever, it was hard for me to wait for morning.

Conana, the green-eyed calico, has been out of sorts since Judy walked out. Judy had worked nights, so she had been home for Conana during the day. Now Conana sat, lonely and forlorn, in the bedroom window, with no one to give her treats or rub her stomach . . . a little like me, maybe.

"I'm trying as hard as I can to find someone who'll love both of us," I told her. "I know it's no fun to be by yourself. Maybe tomorrow . . ."

I had a huge smile ready, but when she barely acknowledged my presence, I changed it to a nod that was shorter than the one she gave me. In the cafeteria, we slid our trays along the serving line, spoke only to the young student working behind the counter and walked our trays to the nearest table.

On the edge of rage, I sugared my coffee before I could look across the table at her. She was looking back at me, and her lips slowly parted in the same smile I got yesterday.

"You're thinking this isn't going to work, aren't you? I can tell." She raised her eyebrows.

Her voice was low and soft, almost a purr. Since I'd never heard her string more than six words together, and that only once, I gawked at her. It wasn't just the words she used, but what the words implied.

"You can tell?" I echoed.

"Who couldn't?" she asked, flashing that same mysterious little smile.

"You knew?" I stuttered. What I meant was, did you know I've been after you because I want you naked in bed with me? Then it struck me that I had cut my part of the conversation down to two one-syllable words. Let her top that, I thought.

"Yes," she answered.

My face turned as red as my running shorts. Was she a mind reader?

She waited for me to speak, tapping faintly on her juice glass with her index finger, and watching my face.

"Eat your breakfast," she said finally. "We'll talk later."

"Later?" I squeaked. "Later?"

"Yes, Mary Ellen, later. We certainly can't talk here."

I began to gobble food, my mind racing. I had a staff meeting after the library closed which meant it'd be after ten before I'd be free. Could I hope she'd meet me that late? She taught math, and I hadn't gotten much higher than the Dewey Decimals, so we had little in common except we both loved women, and I could feel vibes from her that were lifting me off the chair.

"I won't be free for any length of time until after ten tonight . . ."

"Fine," she interrupted, "my place at ten-thirty. Here's my address and phone number. Got to run. I'm late for class."

And she was gone. I stumbled toward my usual morning destination, quickly calculating that if I really pushed the meeting, I could just make it home for a quick shower and change, leave Conana more dry food, and still arrive pretty close to ten-thirty. It was going to be a long day.

When she opened the door, she took my hand and held it until we were both seated on one of two matching two-person couches which I'm sure had some clever name that eluded me at the moment.

"Would you like some wine?" she asked.

I immediately grasped the fact that that would mean she would have to get up and move away from me, which did not at all fit in with my other wishes at the moment.

"No, thanks," I replied, proud of my ability to converse so normally under such extreme pressure.

"Well, then, it's your move, my dear."

A long pause followed, during which I composed myself completely. She waited, unmoving. Finally I said, "I wanted to meet you because I was told you were a lesbian. My friends said you were a runner, didn't talk much, didn't socialize and were living alone. I thought we could become friends if we ran . . . uh, walked, together."

"We've been set up!" she interrupted gleefully. "I was told the same thing about you."

"Set up?" I asked dumbly.

"Yes, I haven't been talkative because I heard you

wouldn't like a chatterbox. Why do you think I've walked my feet to the bone? Would any sane person do that deliberately?"

"Then you were pretending?"

"Pretending? My dear I think our 'sisters' didn't want two single lesbians wandering around, so they fed each of us just enough to get us curious. While you were chasing me, I was chasing you!"

She stood and took my hand again.

Close to morning she leaned on an elbow and began lightly brushing my breasts with her lips. "From now on, the only walking I intend to do is this." And she walked two fingers down my body, stopping when her arm ran out of reach. I claimed her hand with mine and settled it between my legs.

"Now walk in place," I ordered.

She did.

Southern Nights
Laura DeHart Young

Nothing had changed. There was the same tension in the air, a familiar indifference that played over the sound of dinner dishes being put away and drowned out the evening news. Sara peeked through the living-room blinds to find the sun setting in an orange blaze just above the pines. At least that was something.

"Aren't you going to be late?" the mostly disinterested voice asked.

"Maybe. Not for you to worry about."

Sara stepped around the cardboard boxes cluttering the living room. Sitting down on the sofa, she shuffled through the day's mail, trying to ignore the anger that threatened to swallow her. Yes, their relationship was over. It wasn't a shock. She had stayed too long, put up with too much and, in the end, the final blow had struck as hard as all the others. Finding her lover of five years in bed with another friend. Their eyes searing into her like flames against flesh. And the blood that was shed was all her own.

She got up from the sofa and without a word closed the back door behind her. As she slid into the front seat and pulled the belt across her shoulder, she sighed heavily. It would all be over soon. The boxes would be gone. The clothes. The material things that spanned five years and two houses and every birthday, holiday and anniversary celebration in between. In her mind she could already hear the echo of an empty house, her shoes hitting the hardwood floors as she walked the rooms one last time to say goodbye.

She took 75 North into the city. The Atlanta skyline suddenly came into view, stretching ever higher in a glow of bright lights and geometric shapes. It was a dazzling horizon of glass and metal, spheres and pinnacles, towers and pyramids. In the five years she had lived there, she never got tired of the view.

It was too early for the Friday night dance crowd. The bar was almost empty when she walked in. And then she saw her friend's familiar smile — the only sight she knew that soothed the insistent pain pushing from within.

"Hey, baby," Kelly said in her thick, Southern drawl. "I thought you might stand me up. You're never late."

She gave a weak shrug. "Sorry, Kell. Traffic."

"Yeah, right. More like an out-of-control bus named Susan." Kelly leaned into the bar and ordered them both a drink. "She still packin'?"

"Yes. Tomorrow she'll be gone."

Kelly handed her a beer. She threw the wild tangle of auburn hair over one shoulder and stared at her with those brown-black eyes. "I knew I should've smacked the dog shit out of that woman years ago. She treated you like garbage."

That was Kelly, she thought. As blunt as a dull blade. "She did. You were right. Don't you ever get tired of being right?"

"I'm sorry, Sara. This time, I wish I'd been wrong. I only wanted you to be happy."

"I know."

She sat on the only piece of furniture left, other than her bedroom suite. It had been her grandmother's chair — an antique black Boston rocker that had spent most of its first hundred years on a front porch.

As a little girl, she'd sat in the same rocker when she was mad. Mad at her mom, or her brothers or friends. She'd rock so hard that all she could hear was the clump, clump, clump of the chair hitting her grandparents' wood-planked porch. Somehow, it made the anger go away.

The chair clumped now against the bare hardwood floor. But the anger was still there. She didn't even hear the knocking at the door or the familiar voice yelling, "Sara. Hey, Sara." The key turned in the lock. Kelly suddenly strode into the room. Sara wondered how long her friend had been waiting.

"Hey, baby. What's up?"

"Hi, Kell. Not much."

Kelly leaned over and kissed her on the cheek. "I've been poundin' on the door for ten minutes. I got worried, so I let myself in."

"Sorry."

"It's okay."

"There's nowhere for you to sit."

Kelly plopped down on the floor. "No problem. How're you holdin' up?"

"I'm holding."

"You can always hold onto me."

"I'm counting on it."

It seemed that she had always been holding onto Kelly. A year ago, when things were far out of control, the key had turned in the lock then. She remembered the humiliation — how she tried to hide her face as Kelly hugged her.

Kelly's eyes were black with anger. "You okay? Why is it so dark in here?" She flipped on the living room lamp. "Where is she?"

"Gone."

"Look at me."

Sara pivoted halfway.

Kelly reached for her. The strong, gentle hand wrapped itself around her forearm and pulled her closer. "Oh, my God."

Sara could feel Kelly's eyes searching the bruises and cuts on her face. She clenched her teeth, waiting for the angry words. But none came. When she looked up, the dark eyes had turned brown again. The words were comforting and soft.

"You need some ice on that face. Lie down on the sofa. I'll be right back."

Sara lay with her bruises packed in ice. Kelly held her hand and stroked her hair. Tears streamed down her face, warm against cold skin.

"I love you, Sara. You know that. Come and stay with me for as long as you need to."

The glow of Kelly's cigarette illuminated her face. It was a strong face — lined with the worry and weight of her own problems. In a bitter break-up three months earlier, Kelly had lost a child and a lover of eight years.

Sara shifted the ice pack and winced. "I don't deserve to have a friend like you."

Kelly exhaled the pale, gray smoke. "Damn it, Sara. You deserve everything. You're smart, caring and beautiful."

"I'm not beautiful."

Kelly had squeezed her hand. "Bullshit. That's Susan talking. Don't you know how attractive you are? What a wonderful person you are?"

"Maybe if I tried harder —"

"Listen, baby. It's not your fault. There's no excuse for this. You're coming home with me."

That night Sara did go home with Kelly. Two

weeks later, after Susan begged and pleaded for hours each day on the phone, Sara went back. Back to the same problems, the same empty promises, the same abuse. *Abuse.* The word finally had meaning. It sat in the pit of her stomach and made her nauseous.

The rocking chair clumped onto Kelly's sneaker.

"Hey. Watch it. My feet are ugly enough."

"Sorry."

Kelly slid a cigarette out of the foil-wrapped pack. "I ran into Anne last night at the grocery store. Gracie was with her."

"Oh, Kell. I'm so sorry."

"When I lost my daughter, I lost everything." Kelly cleared her throat, got up and walked toward the window. "When that six-year-old child put her hand in mine and looked up at me, I saw in her eyes everything that I was." The cigarette burned orange in the fading light. "I'll never have another relationship again. Never."

"That's premature, Kell. You have your whole life ahead of you."

"I don't want to fall in love again. You're the only person I care about, Sara. The only thing that keeps me going."

"I feel the same way."

Kelly turned on the heel of her boot, her mood suddenly changed. "I'm taking you to dinner tonight."

"Why?"

"Honey, weren't you outside at all today? Spring's in the air, Sara. You know what that means? Beautiful Southern nights — just like tonight. So, let's rock." Kelly smiled broadly. "Without the rocker."

Sara laughed. It felt strange. Laughter had been locked away — distant like the memories. "Thanks, Kell."

"For what?"

"Coming to my rescue again. I thought you might give up on me by this time."

"Baby, don't you know? I'm like gum on your shoe. You just can't get rid of me."

After dinner, they went to Kelly's apartment located south of the city. As Kelly made drinks in the kitchen, she talked about herself, telling stories Sara never grew tired of hearing.

"As a kid, I can remember sittin' at the table in my mom's kitchen. We'd all be so hungry, there'd be one potato left and eight forks reachin' for it at the same time." Kelly laughed over the sound of the blender. "Man, if you stabbed it first, you got up and ran with it."

The old cliché was never more true: she and Kelly were as different as night and day. Kelly was born in rural Georgia — so poor that hunger was not an uncommon sensation. As a teenager, Kelly moved to Alabama to work in the coal mines. Financing her education was a struggle. She worked multiple jobs to pay every bill.

Sara was born in suburban Philadelphia. Her father had been a prominent criminal attorney. Mealtime in her house was spread the length of a grand mahogany table with real silverware and china, crystal stemware and carefully taught manners. College was paid for — along with cars and clothes and summer trips to Europe.

Kelly handed Sara her drink and sat down on the sofa, stretching her long legs in front of her. "Sara, you know that I love you."

"Yes, of course."

Putting her arm around Sara's shoulder, Kelly pulled her close and kissed her. Their lips melted together like rain on a warm night. It was a soft, lingering kiss that seemed to draw the last breath from her lungs. Sara felt only one emotion: love. She knew love took many forms, wore different disguises and, like a chameleon, changed itself when least expected. But she no longer had expectations. They had died long ago. Fear was the only thing she knew — the fear of being hurt again. In her heart, a tiny glow of light was the only spark left. A light of friendship that had shown her the way during a very dark time.

The bedroom was dark; the only light came from the window to her left where the soft glow of a street light outside edged its way across the bed. Sara fell backward as Kelly lay over her — a beautiful shadow against the gray-lit room. Kelly's hands pressed tightly into her own, the weight of her friend's body pinning her against the bed. Suddenly, she froze. She turned her head and winced, her teeth biting into her bottom lip until it bled.

"Baby, what's wrong?"

Sara looked up and remembered. It was Kelly. "I'm sorry. For a moment, I thought —"

Kelly loosened her grip and put her hands alongside Sara's face. "Honey, I'm sorry. I would never hurt you. Never."

"I know." She forced a smile. "I'm okay."

"Listen, I'll just hold you. Okay?"

Sara pulled Kelly's hand to her mouth. She kissed its palm, then placed the strong hand across her breast. "No. Don't stop."

A tongue traced Sara's lips until she found a kiss she wanted to taste forever. Passionate, but gentle. A kiss that drew her deep inside and held her there — on the edge of letting go.

Kelly slid down, unbuttoning Sara's shirt, unhooking her bra — her mouth hungry for Sara's breasts. She closed her eyes and sighed as Kelly's tongue delicately circled her nipples, until each one was pulled slowly into her mouth. Sara felt Kelly's hands at her back — forcing her deeper into Kelly's mouth, her nipples hard inside the curl of Kelly's tongue.

Sara wrapped herself around Kelly's leg, pressing herself tightly against its muscled thigh. As Kelly's palms pressed against her nipples, Sara moved to satisfy herself.

Kelly moved with her, matching the rhythm. "I love the way you move underneath me. Take what you want, baby."

Sara thrust herself hard against Kelly's leg. Her fingernails dug through the shirt into Kelly's back as the first orgasm shuddered through her. She trembled against Kelly, her body still moving — still wanting more.

"You're so sexy."

Sara closed her eyes. She'd never felt sexy before.

As if reading her mind, Kelly said, "You are, Sara. So beautiful."

Sara ran her fingers through Kelly's hair. "But why, Kell? I thought you said —"

"That I never wanted to fall in love again?"

"Yes."

"You're the most important person in my life. You have been for a long time. That's all I know."

Sara kissed the bridge of Kelly's nose. "That's enough."

Hours later, she lay in Kelly's arms. Watching the glow of Kelly's cigarette, she felt a tremendous sense of peace, of being protected and cared for by a friend she knew would never hurt her. She felt safe in Kelly's arms. And she felt loved. It was a different kind of love she never knew existed. A kind of love that remained free of broken promises and empty dreams. And, whatever became of them — whether they were together or apart, friends or life-partners — this one Southern night would live in her heart forever.

Life Models

Diana Simmonds

At three-thirty on a Sunday afternoon, the sound of
a human voice was startling. Startling because,
during the hours — maybe not hours but they felt
like it — that I'd been lying on the veranda peering
over the edge at the ants in the dust below, there
had been no other sound that could remotely be
described as interesting.

To a person whose childhood was spent in a small
country town, the absence of interest on a hot Sunday afternoon wouldn't be remarkable — but a pure,

dark honey-toasted, Ella kind of voice singing "Lady Be Good" would.

I was not then sixteen years old and I had never before heard "Lady Be Good." My mother had some records of Ray Conniff and Billy Vaughn, and I had two records: the Everly Brothers and Elvis — who made me feel hot and strange inside — yet nothing like this soft but penetrating voice and this melancholy song. Not that I knew it was melancholy at the time, but I did know that it made me forget the ants and listen. And shivers of sadness caused the hairs on the back of my neck to stand on end.

Until that moment, the quiet of Sunday afternoon had been made quieter by the scrape of dry grass stem on dry grass stem and the soughing of an un-relieving breeze in the lemon trees and hibiscus. Two streets away in Mrs. Rosenblum's backyard a cockerel crowed occasionally; two streets the other way, the Church of God choir practiced staying roughly in the region of the same tune; but where I was, with my father gone fishing and my mother and grandmother asleep, the depth of silence — and its nothingness — was so thick it made my ears ring. And my heart ached with what I would have described as unbear-able ennui if I'd known what it was. I just knew that on a Sunday afternoon, tears would eventually spontaneously start in the corners of my eyes.

As well as ennui — which, as you may realize, I suffered unknowingly but instinctively — I was also lonely. I was lonely because I was weird. And I was weird because Diane Thompson said so. If I had been a bit braver I might have retorted that in my view it was pretty weird to let Christopher Tugwell stick his

tongue down your throat and squeeze your breasts,
because he had terrible acne and greasy hair. But I
didn't. Instead, when we all went to the movies on
Friday nights, I'd sit beside Diane and Christopher in
the back row and listen to their tongues while
Vernon Patterson sat beside me with his bony red
hands clasped between his bony red knees.

Vernon had a wet tongue and he seemed always
to be trying to feel my tonsils with it. I couldn't
understand why Diane liked it so much, it made me
want to throw up. But one night, while we were
watching a movie with Troy Donahue and Suzanne
Pleshette, I began to understand something.

Troy was tall and skinny like me, but he had
blue eyes and blond hair and when he looked at
Suzanne, he smoldered. And that night I knew how
he felt, because, from the first moment she came
onto the screen, I too had been looking at Suzanne
as he did. And her face was imprinted indelibly on
the insides of my eyelids: her dark curly hair, her
dark blue eyes and the curve of her lips beneath
their pale pink lipstick. When she smiled her teeth
were perfect and the corners of her mouth curled up
and she had impossibly thick black lashes (of course
they were impossible, they were Maybelline, but I
didn't know that then). Then there was her voice. It
wasn't like any other I'd ever heard; it was velvety
and dusky and seemed to come in a chocolate
whisper from somewhere deep in her throat.

That night I heard fast shallow breathing and
realized it was me, then Vernon heard it too and suddenly he lunged and his tongue filled my mouth and
throat. I gagged and, without meaning to, bit down

on its thick, slippery meatiness. Not surprisingly, a
few days later, when Vernon's tongue returned to
normal size and he was able to speak, he told me
he'd decided we should break up.

In truth, although I felt momentarily humiliated, I
didn't mind "breaking up" — something that at least
sounded glamorous and dramatic — because I knew
only too well there was nothing between us to break,
except the convention that you had to have someone
to neck with at the movies. And I didn't even mind
that because now I had Suzanne Pleshette to think
about and it was easier on my own.

Then, one Sunday afternoon, as I watched ants
and waited for my life to begin, I heard the voice
lazily singing "Lady Be Good." It was coming from
the Birdsalls' house. The Birdsalls had recently
divorced and their house had been To Let for three
months. The Birdsalls' divorce hadn't been a topic of
conversation at lunch — my mother would rather die
than mention the "d" word — but the empty state of
their house had been.

"I don't like it, Barry," my mother said. And she
dabbed her mouth with a corner of her napkin. "It's
bad for the street. You should do something about
it."

For once my father didn't sink his neck into his
shoulders and hurry on with his food. Instead he sat
up deliberately straight and propped his knife and
fork on either side of his plate and said, "It's been
let."

"Oh! You didn't tell me."

"Only found out this morning. Jeff Williams at

the real estate office told me. Thought we'd be pleased."

It seemed that my mother was pleased and not pleased, all at once. My grandmother didn't seem to mind one way or the other, just as long as it didn't interfere with her lunch.

"Who's moving in, Dad?"

My mother looked at me with the expression of shock that always came over her face when she remembered she had a daughter. Then she turned to my father. "Yes," she said. "Who *is* moving in?"

"Moved," said my father. "Already in, apparently. Believe she's a dancer."

"She? You mean a single woman? A dancer? Are you *sure*? That can't be right."

At this point you have to remember that we're talking about the '60s which, contrary to popular mythology, were not really "Swinging" at all — at least, not unless you lived in London or San Francisco and it was 1968. Our town was neither of those and anyway, it was 1964. That Sunday afternoon I had begun to understand that if I lived there much longer, I would actually be able to feel myself suffocating, up to my neck in boredom and apathy. And then I'd heard the voice and the song.

I'd got up and made it to the fence on silent bare feet as the jazz-tinged lines of the song drew me on. On tiptoe I was able to peer over quite handily and did so, straight into a face that displaced Suzanne Pleshette in an instant.

"Hi." The voice that belonged to the face and the song still sounded like liquid chocolate and both, I saw, belonged to a golden and stark naked body. "We must be neighbors. I'm Natalie. Come on over and help me housewarm."

"Sure. Give me a minute."

This was the longest and least surly sentence I'd uttered in years. As I walked around to our gate, along the footpath to next door's gate and into the front yard, I wondered what I would say next. Because of Elvis and latterly, Troy Donahue, I'd gotten pretty good at glowering and saying nothing. It helped to be tall, skinny, under-developed and a "tomboy," but now I felt a strong sense of disadvantage and a sudden desire for Cary Grant charm.

Before I reached the side gate it was opened by Natalie who had wrapped herself in a vivid green and blue sarong and was smiling at me. "Hi again," she said. She didn't look a bit like Suzanne Pleshette except that she had deep blue eyes; her hair was sandy-colored and silky straight and she had a smile as wide as her face.

"Hi," I said and wished my voice was deeper. She didn't seem to notice. "I'm Caroline." I put my hand out, hoping I looked sophisticated and not nervous. She took it in both hers and her palms were warm and firm and dry.

"Good to meet you. Would you like something to drink, or a swim maybe — or both?"

The Birdsalls' pool was the talk of the town when they'd built it. This was because it was an irregular shape and pale jade green, surrounded by ferns, palms, lilies and water plants so it looked like a pool in a jungle glade and with a little waterfall at one end that fell into it. My mother had been convinced

it would attract mosquitoes because it wasn't rec-
tangular and tiled in pale blue, but from my bedroom
window, it looked romantic and cool. Now, as Natalie
led me to it, I saw that it *was* romantic and cool —
quite an achievement in our street in high summer. I
felt a fleeting sense of regret for the Birdsalls — that
this beautiful thing had not made them happy.

"What would you like to drink?" I wondered
whether Natalie was a witch and whether this feeling
in my chest was what being bewitched meant.

"What are you having?" My voice sounded deeper
than before and calm. We stood on the deck beside
the pool and I discovered as Natalie smiled up at me
that I was much taller; and I wanted to touch the
line that made the curve of her chin and throat.

"Vodka and tonic." She looked at me with one eye
half closed, as if she was focusing better. "Would you
like one?"

"That would be nice." Without meaning to I
glanced at our house; I couldn't help it. My mother's
view of "drink" was in line with the pamphlets put
out by her Christian Ladies Fellowship Guild; my
father, on the other hand, had said to me before the
end-of-term dance that the odd vodka had never hurt
anyone and what's more couldn't be detected on the
breath.

"Ice?" Natalie was halfway to the house.

"Please," I called softly, hoping, I have to admit,
that my mother would never wake up ever again.

Beside the pool was a low table made of white
painted wooden slats. On either side of it was a
white painted wooden lounger. I sat down; on the
table were a towel and a book, *Madam Bovary*. I

hadn't read it — but then, I'd only just begun reading again after years of refusing to even open a book. Something about the way Suzanne Pleshette made me feel had compelled me to return to books. I picked up this one that belonged to Natalie.

"Have you read it?"

"Not yet."

Natalie twisted an ice tray into a white plastic bucket. "Borrow that copy," she said and it was clear she meant it. "I've read it a thousand times and I just pick it up when I feel like it and start anywhere. You'll love it."

I laid the book back on the table and watched her pour my drink. The splash of vodka was not insulting but it didn't make me feel apprehensive either. She dropped in three ice blocks, a lemon slice and broke the seal of a fresh bottle of tonic water. As she gripped the bottle top the muscles of her arms and stomach tightened and rippled beneath her brown skin.

"There, try that." Natalie held out the tumbler and waited as I tasted the drink. It was sweet and cold and the quinine and lemon puckered my tongue pleasantly.

"It's perfect."

"Good." She topped up her own drink and sat down, raising the glass toward me. Eventually I realized she expected me to touch my glass to hers. I did, they rang like tiny bells and the ice echoed the sound. "Cheers," she said. "And thank you for coming over."

I was lost for a moment because her smile was such a wideness of full and softly defined lips that I couldn't speak. But words came out of my mouth despite me. "Thanks for asking me over," I heard me say. "Sunday afternoons aren't all they're cracked up to be around here." I was amazed at how composed I sounded.

"It *is* very quiet," Natalie observed. She lay back in the lounger, drew up one leg and rested the glass on her knee. "But I like it. It's exactly what I need right now."

I nodded, wondering why and feeling unable to ask. Instead I sipped my drink and said, "I can't wait to leave. I'm going to law school."

"That's wonderful."

I had never before heard such utter conviction expressed in two words. In that moment I knew, without doubt and for the first time, that I *was* going to law school.

"Does your boyfriend mind?"

This time I took a gulp of the drink and almost choked. "I don't have a boyfriend."

She chuckled. "What's wrong with the boys around here?"

I set down my glass and shook my head. "Nothing. It's me. I don't really want a boyfriend."

Natalie nodded. "I see."

"No, you don't," I said earnestly. I could feel my words and thoughts running away from me, maybe it was the vodka, I didn't care. "The thing is, my best friend is *in love* with Elvis but I want to *be* Elvis..." I stopped then, shocked by this truth that I didn't even know I knew until I heard it spoken. I stared at the blue-tinged drink in my glass, waiting for Natalie to laugh or say something dismissive.

Instead she said, "How old are you?"

"I'll be sixteen in two months." Again I waited, this time for her to say something about crushes and going through phases as Miss Fordham had explained them last term, but she didn't. She drained her glass, looked at mine, said, "Drink up, let's swim." Stood and let her sarong drop to the deck.

To this day I have trouble spelling exhilaration — never quite sure whether it's with an *e* or an *a* — but since that day I've known without doubt what it meant. I watched her dive in and saw her naked body as sets of striated ripples beneath the surface. Maybe the vodka gave me courage, or maybe I was growing up. I pulled off my shirt and jeans, hid my sensible white cotton knickers inside them and before I hit the water I was in love.

After that first Sunday afternoon, my life revolved in a blur of bewildered happiness around Natalie's schedule at the Monsoon Nite Club and Cabaret. Did I mention that she was an exotic dancer and jazz singer? No, but my father hadn't either, you'll recall — at least, not over Sunday lunch.

My mother very nearly fainted when she found out and very nearly did so again when she discovered that I'd already met Natalie. And she actually did faint when, for the first time in their married life, my father told her in a voice I'd never heard before, to "stop being a fool and leave the girl alone. She's growing up and you can't stop her," after she'd forbade me to return to the Birdsalls' house.

That summer Natalie celebrated her twenty-fifth birthday. Twenty-five was impossibly remote to me then and when Diane Thompson crossly asked, "Why on earth are you her best friend, Caro? I really don't understand," I could only shrug in sympathetic confusion. And when Natalie's Saturday afternoon pool parties became *the* place for the town's fast young set (my mother's description, by the way), Diane was even crosser and took to calling me "Natalie's toy poodle."

It might have stung if I'd been less than completely happy and if I had any time to be upset by Diane but, instead of waiting for her to call, I'd sleep in until close to midday, then slip over to Natalie's and have the coffee on by the time she appeared, sleepy-eyed and tousled and sniffing the air. On the third day after Sunday, or thereabouts, she gave me a warm, sweet-scented kiss on the cheek by way of greeting and, thereafter, each day I would inhale the fresh-baked-cookie smell of her skin and hair and almost die of elation.

She had an old car that squeaked and rattled over the rough roads around our town. Its front seat was an unbroken bench of dark green, worn leather and the steering wheel was ivory-colored and had an inner metal ring for the horn. She drove one-handed, with her other arm on the window sill and, on the passenger side, I stretched out — like Elvis — behind a pair of mirrored shades she'd found for me at Woolworths. We visited every attraction, from the plow museum to the district's oldest working cider press, during those afternoons. But more often than not, we'd lie by the pool and talk.

My life story didn't take all that long, but she seemed to want to know every detail of it anyway. And even more surprisingly, she seemed to want to know what I thought about things. Most of the time I didn't know whether I even had an opinion until she asked me, but I soon got the hang of it — thinking, considering, analyzing, trying out a thought, modifying it, listening to her, modifying it again and then, increasingly, arguing it out until we were both satisfied. Reluctantly, late in the afternoon, I would go home flushed beneath my tan, drunk on ideas and the excitement of debate, scarcely able to bear being deprived of it until the next day. And late at night, I'd hear her car as she returned from the Monsoon, and I'd wish with all my heart that I was older.

As it happened, my sixteenth birthday fell a week before her twenty-fifth and it was decided — Natalie decided — that we would have a joint party. It was to be my very first birthday party, as my mother had never gone along with that kind of frivolity; while for his part, each year, my father had simply slipped me a steadily increasing sum in smooth new notes and told me not to spend it all at once. He had expressed delight at the idea of the party and immediately went over to the Birdsalls' house to check what he could do. My mother pressed her lips tight until they were white, which was better than the alternative.

On the morning of the party, my father disappeared early, whistling. Meanwhile, my mother's silence deepened into profound disbelief and something she might have recognized as anger if she could ever have admitted to such a passion. I felt sorry for

them both from the Olympian height of my own pre-
occupation: sorry that they had nothing like my
happiness, that my mother was so allergic to love and
that my father had been so cheated of it. These
concepts were the result of hours lying beside Natalie
in the dappled sunshine by the pool, talking and — I
understood later — being talked into seeing them as
human beings; and so I felt compassion for them for
the first time and my surliness had disappeared, to
my mother's consternation and my father's evident
delight. Listening to Natalie — to the story of how
she came to be in our town — I felt much much
more; but it remained locked in my heart, safe from
the corrosive effects of common knowledge.

When my father returned from his expedition with
strings of party lights, eight bags of ice, a galvanized
iron bath to put it in and a huge barbecue borrowed
from a friend who attended the same lodge, I began
to get an inkling that this Saturday night could be
special. Natalie had taken the night off from the
Monsoon and most of the staff had promised to come
on to the party when they knocked off. The "fast
young set" had been agonizing over their outfits for
the previous fortnight and even I had relented and
allowed Natalie to take me shopping.

I'd balked at a dress but gave in to a shirt —
Natalie called it a blouse — in the colors of a psyche-
delic, glitter-encrusted, chiffon rainbow. It had wide
floating sleeves which seemed to create their own
breeze and ended in floppy, floaty frills that matched
the floppy floaty frills where I'd honestly have preferred a collar. Natalie found it at Dorothee: Boutique

Chic — real name Dorothy and she'd sold Ladies Modes before Mary Quant turned dress shops upside down.

"Fabulous," Natalie said as I stood in front of the mirror poking doubtfully at the frill, which seemed to want to fall open where my breasts began. "We'll get you some white jeans and you'll look great. Trust me."

And of course, I had. At the party I didn't look like Diane and the other girls, I didn't look like the smart women who came from the club and I certainly didn't look like my mother and the other ladies who occupied a table at one end of the pool and didn't move all evening for fear of catching syphilis; but I did, I finally realized, look like me and I was content with that.

My father and two of his Lodge cronies managed the barbecue and kept up a constant supply of black-edged steaks, burst sausages and squashy white rolls. After beginning with Perry Como and Jim Reeves, Maurie — the DJ from the Monsoon — arrived with a case of records and in minutes the Birdsalls' backyard was transformed into a tiny outpost of the Swinging '60s.

My father had come into the garden as twilight fell carrying a cardboard box of twelve bottles of champagne. "I think this is your first, Caroline," he'd said, smiling at me. "And I hope it isn't your last. Happy birthday, dear."

So I drank champagne for the first time, inhaled the bubbles and coughed, grinned as Natalie laughed at me and prayed that this night and this summer would never end. I had never voluntarily danced with

anyone before but I wanted to dance with her. I
watched her moving like a movie star as she jived
and twisted and Madisoned with almost every man in
town. And I danced, for old times' sake, with Vernon
Patterson until he grabbed me and pulled me against
his erection and I understood there was such a thing
as too much fun.

In the Birdsalls' kitchen I poured myself more
champagne and leaned against the sink, pondering
the wreckage and wondering who was currently bene-
fiting from Natalie's *joie de vivre.* Then the door
opened and she was there.

"How're you coping?" she asked, setting her glass
down with difficulty amid the detritus.

"Brilliantly," I said. "This is the best night of my
life and I want to thank you for it."

"My pleasure. Would you like your birthday
present now?"

"You bet."

"Come with me."

In her bedroom she closed the door and held out
a package to me and I looked at it, cradled in her
two hands. I'd never been given a present before that
wasn't useful (school books, sensible underwear,
sewing kits, you know the kind of thing) and I
wasn't sure of the protocol. She held her hands a
little farther toward me, as if she were holding a bit
of apple and I was a skittish horse. I took the package and stood, paralyzed, in the shadowy, flower-
scented candlelight of Natalie's bedroom.

"Open it, you goose," she said, and her voice was
tender and amused. At that moment, more than anything in the world, I wanted to tell her that I loved

her. But of course I didn't. Instead I began to un-
wrap the layers of crispy white paper until I found a
small velvet bag whose neck was tied with a length
of silver satin ribbon. I loosened the ribbon and up-
ended the bag into the palm of my hand. Out
slithered a thick silver chain and hanging from it was
half of a fat silver coin, roughly snapped in two and
whose other half, I knew, was always around
Natalie's neck.

My heart stopped for a second as I held up the
chain and understood what she had given me. Then I
spoke, the first honest and brave words of my adult
life. "I love you."

"I know." Her smile had gone and her face was
somber, older, in the flickering golden light of the
candle. She held out her hand to me and I took the
two steps that ended with her arms around my neck.
"Sweetheart," she whispered. "I think we've waited
long enough." And she put her hand on the back of
my neck and drew me down to her wide, smiling,
generous mouth.

Natalie locked her bedroom door on the party and
the rest of the world, and we became like those two
silver halves: different but inseparably linked and,
when together, complete.

She led me to her bed and I fell upon her, de-
vouring the sweetness and softness that her body had
always promised. Her tongue explored mine and I
filled my mouth with her. Her breasts and skin were
what I had dreamed of, yet I was awake and we
were hungry for each other. She tore my chiffon frills
and her teeth sank into my flesh. As she pushed into
my virginity with her fingers and tongue, I in-

stinctively opened before her and cried out, but the pain she caused me was blissful and I could only beg for more and clasp her close and tight.

Before long, she whispered in my ear, "Fuck me." And the constraint I had felt melted in a hot rush of desire. As I traveled every crevice and plane of her body my tears were another wetness that mingled with hers and I plumbed her salt-sweet depths like a starving ruffian. As my tongue discovered each new softness I knew I had hungered for it and waited for it and craved it all my life; and I savored her and filled myself with her and still could not get enough as I felt her clasp and enclose me as I moved to the internal rhythms of her body. And we pushed on into each other, our fingers in each other's mouths, our sweat slippery and our eyes and hands all-consuming as sensation and pleasure and hearts collided and fused in trembling orgasm and adoration.

I have worn both halves of the coin around my neck now for twenty years. I wear them in court and, although I am not otherwise superstitious, I've never lost a case when they've hung at the base of my throat, beneath my formal white court shirts. Natalie gave me my half because, she said, it rightfully belonged to a soulmate. And, she said, I was hers and she was mine — unlikely though it may have seemed to the rest of the world at that point. But neither the world nor we had time to discover whether or not she was right. The illness which had caused her to retreat to the obscurity of our town for a while reemerged and, within two years, she was dead.

She believed that we go full circle in our lives and end up — if we're lucky — with what we first sought and found. She said that when a strange "boy-girl" poked her head over the fence to see who was singing, her heart had completed its full circle and she felt at home. I can only say that I had never known home or the concept of perfect circles before Natalie.

Just before she died, she gave me her half of the coin and made me promise that I'd keep it until I felt the circle closing on a soulmate once again. There surely can't be that many blue-eyed, chocolate-voiced, generously beautiful beings and the passion they bring with them in one person's lifetime; yet I still feel hopeful whenever I hear Ella's "Lady Be Good."

About the Authors

LAURA ADAMS — Once a Girl Guide, always a Girl Guide. Earnest and prepared, and loving the company of the other girls, Laura, at the age of twelve, declared in her journal that she would like to remain twelve all her life. At nineteen, loving the company of other women, she recorded in her journal that she'd always like to be nineteen. Looking back from thirty-something she tells Journal, an overly fluffy tabby who adopted Laura during the Broken Icebox/Salmon Glut of 1993, that no one could pay her enough to be nineteen again. She wouldn't want to relive most of the experiences that led her to knowing what she knows now, especially the years she spent committing the number of isomers of uranium to memory. It is also far too handy to be able to point out constellations on dates, amaze her friends by demonstrating how sodium bicarbonate (also known as baking soda) dumped in a slow drain and rinsed down with vinegar can improve the plumbing, and explain to perfect strangers on mass transit that it is possible to spend a year by yourself in a remote observatory and come home perfectly sane. Laura's first book for Naiad is *Night Vision* and her next will be *Christabel*. Laura Adams is the closely guarded *nom de plume* of a famous lesbian romance writer.

SAXON BENNETT lives in Phoenix, Arizona, where she is passionately convinced that reading, writing and long runs in the desert make for the perfect day.

JACKIE CALHOUN lives with Diane and her cat along the Fox River, an hour away from the family cottage in the heart of Wisconsin. She has two daughters and two granddaughters to her credit. Calhoun is an avid reader, a lover of classical music and an environmentalist. She is also the author of *Lifestyles, Second Chance, Sticks and Stones, Friends and Lovers, Triple Exposure, Changes, Love or Money,* and *Seasons of the Heart*. She has stories in four Naiad anthologies. When not writing, Calhoun works in an antique mall.

KATE CALLOWAY was born and raised in Southern California which is probably why she's so drawn to the beauty of Oregon, the setting for her Cassidy James mystery series. She and her lover and two cats spend their time between the two states, playing as much as possible. In addition to writing novels, Kate teaches, writes songs, dabbles in poetry, and wines and dines her friends with great abandon. She is currently working on the sixth Cassidy James mystery.

KAYE DAVIS is a criminalist in a Texas Department of Public Safety regional crime laboratory with nineteen years of experience. Her areas of expertise include the analysis of drugs, the examination of paint samples and the comparison of shoe print and tire track evidence. She has testified in court over three hundred times and has participated in numerous crime scene investigations. Kaye's first Maris Middleton mystery, *Devil's Leg Crossing*, was published by Naiad in 1997. The second in the series, *Possessions*, will be published by Naiad in 1998.

LYN DENISON was a librarian before becoming a full-time writer. Her partner is also a librarian, which just goes to prove that tidying books is not the only thing that goes on between library shelves. Lyn lives with her partner in Brisbane, the capital city of Queensland, Australia's Sunshine State. Apart from writing she loves reading, cross stitching and modern country music. Occasionally she ventures out line dancing which even she will admit is not a pretty sight.

CATHERINE ENNIS enjoys writing about things she enjoys. Her novels reflect the environment and culture of the area in which she has spent most of her adult years . . . New Orleans and southern Louisiana in general. The diversity of her characters matches the diversity of her many friends who encourage as well as inspire her writing.

PENNY HAYES was born in Johnson City, New York, in February 1940. As a child she lived on a farm near Binghamton, New York. She later attended college in Utica, Buffalo, and Huntington, WV, graduating with degrees in art and elementary and special education. She has made her living teaching in both New York State and in southern West Virginia. She presently resides in mid-state New York. Ms. Hayes' interests include backpacking, mountain climbing, canoeing, traveling, reading, gardening and building small barns. Her novels include *The Long Trail, Yellowthroat, Montana Feathers, Grassy Flats, Kathleen O'Donald,* and *Now and Then.* She has also written short stories for *The Erotic Naiad, The Romantic Naiad, The Mysterious Naiad, The First Time Ever,* and *Dancing in the Dark.* She is presently working on her seventh novel *(City Lights, Country Candles)* scheduled for publication by Naiad Press in March 1998.

PEGGY J. HERRING is a native Texan who lives on seven acres of mesquite with her lover of twenty-one years. She is the author of Once More with Feeling, Love's Harvest and *Hot Check.* Her next novel, *A Moment's Indiscretion*, will be released by Naiad Press in 1998.

LINDA HILL is the author of two recent Naiad Press novels, *Never Say Never,* and *Class Reunion.* Her third novel, *Just Yesterday*, will be released in 1998. Linda lives in the Boston area.

BARBARA JOHNSON's "Lady in Waiting" was inspired by B.L., who, many years ago, actually phrased the first line of the story. And much love to K.D., who, after reading it, took the story beyond the printed page. It's the women in her life who keep Barbara writing.

FRANKIE J. JONES grew up between the soybean rows and cotton stalks of Southeast Missouri, better known to its inhabitants as the Bootheel. She spent most of her three-year enlistment in the Army in Germany where she met her life partner Peggy J. Herring. They currently live in South Texas as far away from cotton stalks as Frankie can get. When not working or writing, Frankie likes to spend time reading, metal detecting and researching the numerous shipwrecks off the Texas coastline.

KARIN KALLMAKER was born in 1960 and raised by her loving, middle-class parents in California's Central Valley. The physician's Statement of Live Birth plainly states "Sex: Female" and "Cry: Lusty." Both are still true. From a normal childhood and equally unremarkable public school adolescence, she went on to obtain an ordinary Bachelor's degree from the California State University at Sacramento. At the age of 16, eyes wide open, she fell into the arms of her first and only sweetheart. Ten years later, after seeing the film *Desert Hearts,* her sweetheart descended on the Berkeley Public Library determined to find some of "those" books. "Rule, Jane" led to "Lesbianism—Fiction" and then on to book after self-affirming book by and about lesbians. These books were the encouragement Karin needed to forget the so-called "mainstream" and spin her first romance for lesbians. That manuscript became her first Naiad Press book, *In Every Port.* She now lives in Oakland with that very same sweetheart; she is a one-woman woman. The happily-ever-after couple became mothers of one quite remarkable child in 1995 and celebrated their Twentieth Anniversary in 1997. In addition to *In Every Port*, she has authored the best-selling *Touchwood, Paperback Romance, Car Pool, Painted Moon, Wild Things* and *Embrace in Motion*. In 1998, look for *Making Up for Lost Time*.

LEE LYNCH has published ten books with Naiad Press, including *Cactus Love* and *The Swashbuckler.* Her most recent publication, edited with Akia Woods, is *Off the Rag, Lesbians Writing on Menopause*. Her column, "The Amazon Trail" appears in a dozen newspapers. *Girlfriends Magazine* is carrying her serialized novel *Country Dyke Tales*. Lee lives in rural Oregon and supports herself with social service work.

MARIANNE MARTIN currently resides in Ann Arbor, Michigan, as a writer and photographer. After many years of teaching in the public school system, she turned her hobbies into a career, first as a photo-journalist with *The Michigan Women's Times*. An athlete since childhood, she has successfully coached basketball and softball at the high school and amateur levels, and field hockey at the collegiate level. Together with her father, she is in the process of designing and building her own home. The experience, despite uncountable splinters and bruises, has taught her more about herself than any other. Her first novel, *Legacy of Love,* will be released by Naiad Press in December 1997.

JANET E. McCLELLAN is the Chief of Police in a small mid-western town. She began her career in law enforcement at age nineteen. During the next twenty-six years she worked as a narcotics investigator, patrol officer, detective, college professor and prison administrator. All of which her mother refers to as her checkered past. When not writing mysteries, she spends her time serving and protecting her small community. For relaxation and inspiration she travels and investigates the mysteries of Dallas, Texas; Kansas City, Missouri; and Eagles Nest, New Mexico. Her first book, *K.C. Bomber*, featuring Detective Tru North, has been published by Naiad Press. Her second novel, *Penn Valley Phoenix*, will be published in May 1998.

ANN O'LEARY was born in Melbourne, Australia, and lives there in domestic bliss with her partner. After many years working in film production and advertising, Ann is now a full-time writer.

TRACEY RICHARDSON was born in Windsor, Ontario, just a short hop from Detroit. She has previously contributed to *Dancing in the Dark* and is the author of the romance *Northern Blue* and the mystery *Last Rites*. Her next mystery will be published by Naiad in 1998.

LISA SHAPIRO is the author of *The Color of Winter* and *Sea to Shining Sea*, both published by Naiad. Her short story, "Familiar Fruit" appeared in *Dancing in the Dark*, and her reviews of romance novels are published in *The Lesbian Review of Books*. She shares a home in Portsmouth, New Hampshire, with Lynne D'Orsay, her lover and life-partner to whom she dedicates every word.

DIANA SIMMONDS is a "new Australian" — Born in London, brought up in Kenya and finally fetching up beside the Pacific on the southern outskirts of Sydney. She is a journalist, editor and spare-time writer. She has written a number of books on subjects ranging from Doris Day to Princess Diana. She is the author of *Heart on Fire* and *Forty Love,* both published by Naiad.

Though **JULIA WATTS** is the proud owner of several tattoos, she runs in terror at the sight of a pair of eyebrow tweezers. A native of rural Southeastern Kentucky, Watts is the author of two novels, *Wildwood Flowers* (Naiad Press, 1996) and *Phases of the Moon* (1997). This year, Watts's writing of lesbian and feminist fiction set in Kentucky earned her a grant from the Kentucky Foundation for Women. She dedicates "Girl Talk" to Thelma Wysong Windham Hicks, who, though she has never given the author a makeover, nevertheless served as the inspiration for this story.

PAT WELCH lives and works in the San Francisco Bay area, where she writes the Helen Black mystery series for Naiad Press. Her fifth novel in the series, *Smoke and Mirrors,* was released in November of 1996. She is currently at work on the sixth entry in the series, titled *Fallen from Grace.* A Southern Lady transplanted to the West Coast, she can be found in her natural habitat of bookstores and coffee shops in Berkeley when she's not writing her Great American Novel.

LAURA DeHART YOUNG currently has three romance novels published by Naiad Press: *There Will Be*

No Goodbyes, Family Secrets, and *Love on the Line.* Her fourth book, *Private Passions,* will be published by Naiad in 1998. Laura lives in Atlanta, Georgia, with her best friend and her ever-faithful pug, Dudley.

A few of the publications of
THE NAIAD PRESS, INC.
P.O. Box 10543 • Tallahassee, Florida 32302
Phone (850) 539-5965
Toll-Free Order Number: 1-800-533-1973
Mail orders welcome. Please include 15% postage.
Write or call for our free catalog which also features an
incredible selection of lesbian videos.

LADY BE GOOD edited by Barbara Grier and Christine Cassidy.
Erotic stories by Naiad Press authors. 288 pp.   ISBN 1-56280-180-5 $14.95

CHAIN LETTER by Claire McNab. 288 pp. 9th Carol Ashton
mystery.   ISBN 1-56280-181-3   11.95

NIGHT VISION by Laura Adams. 256 pp. Erotic fantasy romance
by "famous" author.   ISBN 1-56280-182-1   11.95

SEA TO SHINING SEA by Lisa Shapiro. 256 pp. Unable to resist
the raging passion . . .   ISBN 1-56280-177-5   11.95

THIRD DEGREE by Kate Calloway. 224 pp. 3rd Cassidy James
mystery.   ISBN 1-56280-185-6   11.95

WHEN THE DANCING STOPS by Therese Szymanski. 272 pp.
1st Brett Higgins mystery.   ISBN 1-56280-186-4   11.95

PHASES OF THE MOON by Julia Watts. 192 pp. . . . . hungry
for everything life has to offer.   ISBN 1-56280-176-7   11.95

BABY IT'S COLD by Jaye Maiman. 256 pp. 5th Robin Miller
mystery.   ISBN 1-56280-156-2   10.95

CLASS REUNION by Linda Hill. 176 pp. The girl from her past . . .
                                                ISBN 1-56280-178-3   11.95

DREAM LOVER by Lyn Denison. 224 pp. A soft, sensuous,
romantic fantasy.   ISBN 1-56280-173-1   11.95

FORTY LOVE by Diana Simmonds. 288 pp. Joyous, heart-
warming romance.   ISBN 1-56280-171-6   11.95

IN THE MOOD by Robbi Sommers. 160 pp. The queen of
erotic tension!   ISBN 1-56280-172-4   11.95

SWIMMING CAT COVE by Lauren Douglas. 192 pp. 2nd
Allison O'Neil Mystery.   ISBN 1-56280-168-6   11.95

THE LOVING LESBIAN by Claire McNab and Sharon Gedan.
240 pp. Explore the experiences that make lesbian love unique.
                                                ISBN 1-56280-169-4   14.95

COURTED by Celia Cohen. 160 pp. Sparkling romantic
encounter.   ISBN 1-56280-166-X   11.95

SEASONS OF THE HEART by Jackie Calhoun. 240 pp. Romance
through the years.   ISBN 1-56280-167-8   11.95

K. C. BOMBER by Janet McClellan. 208 pp. 1st Tru North
mystery.   ISBN 1-56280-157-0   11.95

LAST RITES by Tracey Richardson. 192 pp. 1st Stevie Houston
mystery.   ISBN 1-56280-164-3   11.95

EMBRACE IN MOTION by Karin Kallmaker. 256 pp. A whirlwind
love affair.   ISBN 1-56280-165-1   11.95

HOT CHECK by Peggy J. Herring. 192 pp. Will workaholic Alice
fall for guitarist Ricky?   ISBN 1-56280-163-5   11.95

OLD TIES by Saxon Bennett. 176 pp. Can Cleo surrender to a
passionate new love?   ISBN 1-56280-159-7   11.95

LOVE ON THE LINE by Laura DeHart Young. 176 pp. Will Stef
win Kay's heart?   ISBN 1-56280-162-7   11.95

DEVIL'S LEG CROSSING by Kaye Davis. 192 pp. 1st Maris Middleton
mystery.   ISBN 1-56280-158-9   11.95

COSTA BRAVA by Marta Balletbo Coll. 144 pp. Read the book,
see the movie!   ISBN 1-56280-153-8   11.95

MEETING MAGDALENE & OTHER STORIES by
Marilyn Freeman. 144 pp. Read the book, see the movie!
                                              ISBN 1-56280-170-8   11.95

SECOND FIDDLE by Kate Calloway. 208 pp. P.I. Cassidy James'
second case.   ISBN 1-56280-169-6   11.95

LAUREL by Isabel Miller. 128 pp. By the author of the beloved
Patience and Sarah.   ISBN 1-56280-146-5   10.95

LOVE OR MONEY by Jackie Calhoun. 240 pp. The romance of
real life.   ISBN 1-56280-147-3   10.95

SMOKE AND MIRRORS by Pat Welch. 224 pp. 5th Helen Black
Mystery.   ISBN 1-56280-143-0   10.95

DANCING IN THE DARK edited by Barbara Grier & Christine
Cassidy. 272 pp. Erotic love stories by Naiad Press authors.
                                              ISBN 1-56280-144-9   14.95

TIME AND TIME AGAIN by Catherine Ennis. 176 pp. Passionate
love affair.   ISBN 1-56280-145-7   10.95

PAXTON COURT by Diane Salvatore. 256 pp. Erotic and wickedly
funny contemporary tale about the business of learning to live
together.   ISBN 1-56280-114-7   10.95

INNER CIRCLE by Claire McNab. 208 pp. 8th Carol Ashton
Mystery.   ISBN 1-56280-135-X   11.95

LESBIAN SEX: AN ORAL HISTORY by Susan Johnson.
240 pp. Need we say more?   ISBN 1-56280-142-2   14.95

WILD THINGS by Karin Kallmaker. 240 pp. By the undisputed
mistress of lesbian romance.   ISBN 1-56280-139-2   11.95

THE GIRL NEXT DOOR by Mindy Kaplan. 208 pp. Just what
you'd expect.   ISBN 1-56280-140-6   11.95

NOW AND THEN by Penny Hayes. 240 pp. Romance on the
westward journey.   ISBN 1-56280-121-X   11.95

HEART ON FIRE by Diana Simmonds. 176 pp. The romantic and
erotic rival of *Curious Wine.*   ISBN 1-56280-152-X   11.95

DEATH AT LAVENDER BAY by Lauren Wright Douglas. 208 pp.
1st Allison O'Neil Mystery.   ISBN 1-56280-085-X   11.95

YES I SAID YES I WILL by Judith McDaniel. 272 pp. Hot
romance by famous author.   ISBN 1-56280-138-4   11.95

FORBIDDEN FIRES by Margaret C. Anderson. Edited by Mathilda
Hills. 176 pp. Famous author's "unpublished" Lesbian romance.
                                             ISBN 1-56280-123-6   21.95

SIDE TRACKS by Teresa Stores. 160 pp. Gender-bending
Lesbians on the road.   ISBN 1-56280-122-8   10.95

HOODED MURDER by Annette Van Dyke. 176 pp. 1st Jessie
Batelle Mystery.   ISBN 1-56280-134-1   10.95

WILDWOOD FLOWERS by Julia Watts. 208 pp. Hilarious and
heart-warming tale of true love.   ISBN 1-56280-127-9   10.95

NEVER SAY NEVER by Linda Hill. 224 pp. Rule #1: Never get involved
with . . .   ISBN 1-56280-126-0   10.95

THE SEARCH by Melanie McAllester. 240 pp. Exciting top cop
Tenny Mendoza case.   ISBN 1-56280-150-3   10.95

THE WISH LIST by Saxon Bennett. 192 pp. Romance through
the years.   ISBN 1-56280-125-2   10.95

FIRST IMPRESSIONS by Kate Calloway. 208 pp. P.I. Cassidy
James' first case.   ISBN 1-56280-133-3   10.95

OUT OF THE NIGHT by Kris Bruyer. 192 pp. Spine-tingling
thriller.   ISBN 1-56280-120-1   10.95

NORTHERN BLUE by Tracey Richardson. 224 pp. Police recruits
Miki & Miranda — passion in the line of fire. ISBN 1-56280-118-X   10.95

LOVE'S HARVEST by Peggy J. Herring. 176 pp. by the author of
Once More With Feeling.   ISBN 1-56280-117-1   10.95

THE COLOR OF WINTER by Lisa Shapiro. 208 pp. Romantic
love beyond your wildest dreams.   ISBN 1-56280-116-3   10.95

FAMILY SECRETS by Laura DeHart Young. 208 pp. Enthralling
romance and suspense.   ISBN 1-56280-119-8   10.95

INLAND PASSAGE by Jane Rule. 288 pp. Tales exploring conventional & unconventional relationships.   ISBN 0-930044-56-8   10.95

DOUBLE BLUFF by Claire McNab. 208 pp. 7th Carol Ashton Mystery.   ISBN 1-56280-096-5   10.95

BAR GIRLS by Lauran Hoffman. 176 pp. See the movie, read the book!   ISBN 1-56280-115-5   10.95

THE FIRST TIME EVER edited by Barbara Grier & Christine Cassidy. 272 pp. Love stories by Naiad Press authors.   ISBN 1-56280-086-8   14.95

MISS PETTIBONE AND MISS McGRAW by Brenda Weathers. 208 pp. A charming ghostly love story.   ISBN 1-56280-151-1   10.95

CHANGES by Jackie Calhoun. 208 pp. Involved romance and relationships.   ISBN 1-56280-083-3   10.95

FAIR PLAY by Rose Beecham. 256 pp. 3rd Amanda Valentine Mystery.   ISBN 1-56280-081-7   10.95

PAYBACK by Celia Cohen. 176 pp. A gripping thriller of romance, revenge and betrayal.   ISBN 1-56280-084-1   10.95

THE BEACH AFFAIR by Barbara Johnson. 224 pp. Sizzling summer romance/mystery/intrigue.   ISBN 1-56280-090-6   10.95

GETTING THERE by Robbi Sommers. 192 pp. Nobody does it like Robbi!   ISBN 1-56280-099-X   10.95

FINAL CUT by Lisa Haddock. 208 pp. 2nd Carmen Ramirez Mystery.   ISBN 1-56280-088-4   10.95

FLASHPOINT by Katherine V. Forrest. 256 pp. A Lesbian blockbuster!   ISBN 1-56280-079-5   10.95

CLAIRE OF THE MOON by Nicole Conn. Audio Book —Read by Marianne Hyatt.   ISBN 1-56280-113-9   16.95

FOR LOVE AND FOR LIFE: INTIMATE PORTRAITS OF LESBIAN COUPLES by Susan Johnson. 224 pp.   ISBN 1-56280-091-4   14.95

DEVOTION by Mindy Kaplan. 192 pp. See the movie — read the book!   ISBN 1-56280-093-0   10.95

SOMEONE TO WATCH by Jaye Maiman. 272 pp. 4th Robin Miller Mystery.   ISBN 1-56280-095-7   10.95

GREENER THAN GRASS by Jennifer Fulton. 208 pp. A young woman — a stranger in her bed.   ISBN 1-56280-092-2   10.95

TRAVELS WITH DIANA HUNTER by Regine Sands. Erotic lesbian romp. Audio Book (2 cassettes)   ISBN 1-56280-107-4   16.95

CABIN FEVER by Carol Schmidt. 256 pp. Sizzling suspense and passion.   ISBN 1-56280-089-1   10.95

THERE WILL BE NO GOODBYES by Laura DeHart Young. 192 pp. Romantic love, strength, and friendship.   ISBN 1-56280-103-1   10.95

FAULTLINE by Sheila Ortiz Taylor. 144 pp. Joyous comic
lesbian novel.   ISBN 1-56280-108-2   9.95

OPEN HOUSE by Pat Welch. 176 pp. 4th Helen Black Mystery.
                                                  ISBN 1-56280-102-3   10.95

ONCE MORE WITH FEELING by Peggy J. Herring. 240 pp.
Lighthearted, loving romantic adventure.   ISBN 1-56280-089-2   10.95

FOREVER by Evelyn Kennedy. 224 pp. Passionate romance — love
overcoming all obstacles.   ISBN 1-56280-094-9   10.95

WHISPERS by Kris Bruyer. 176 pp. Romantic ghost story
                                                  ISBN 1-56280-082-5   10.95

NIGHT SONGS by Penny Mickelbury. 224 pp. 2nd Gianna Maglione
Mystery.   ISBN 1-56280-097-3   10.95

GETTING TO THE POINT by Teresa Stores. 256 pp. Classic
southern Lesbian novel.   ISBN 1-56280-100-7   10.95

PAINTED MOON by Karin Kallmaker. 224 pp. Delicious
Kallmaker romance.   ISBN 1-56280-075-2   11.95

THE MYSTERIOUS NAIAD edited by Katherine V. Forrest &
Barbara Grier. 320 pp. Love stories by Naiad Press authors.
                                                  ISBN 1-56280-074-4   14.95

DAUGHTERS OF A CORAL DAWN by Katherine V. Forrest.
240 pp. Tenth Anniversay Edition.   ISBN 1-56280-104-X   11.95

BODY GUARD by Claire McNab. 208 pp. 6th Carol Ashton
Mystery.   ISBN 1-56280-073-6   11.95

CACTUS LOVE by Lee Lynch. 192 pp. Stories by the beloved
storyteller.   ISBN 1-56280-071-X   9.95

SECOND GUESS by Rose Beecham. 216 pp. 2nd Amanda Valentine
Mystery.   ISBN 1-56280-069-8   9.95

A RAGE OF MAIDENS by Lauren Wright Douglas. 240 pp. 6th Caitlin
Reece Mystery.   ISBN 1-56280-068-X   10.95

TRIPLE EXPOSURE by Jackie Calhoun. 224 pp. Romantic drama
involving many characters.   ISBN 1-56280-067-1   10.95

UP, UP AND AWAY by Catherine Ennis. 192 pp. Delightful
romance.   ISBN 1-56280-065-5   11.95

PERSONAL ADS by Robbi Sommers. 176 pp. Sizzling short
stories.   ISBN 1-56280-059-0   11.95

CROSSWORDS by Penny Sumner. 256 pp. 2nd Victoria Cross
Mystery.   ISBN 1-56280-064-7   9.95

SWEET CHERRY WINE by Carol Schmidt. 224 pp. A novel of
suspense.   ISBN 1-56280-063-9   9.95

CERTAIN SMILES by Dorothy Tell. 160 pp. Erotic short stories.
                                                  ISBN 1-56280-066-3   9.95

EDITED OUT by Lisa Haddock. 224 pp. 1st Carmen Ramirez
Mystery.   ISBN 1-56280-077-9   9.95

WEDNESDAY NIGHTS by Camarin Grae. 288 pp. Sexy
adventure.   ISBN 1-56280-060-4   10.95

SMOKEY O by Celia Cohen. 176 pp. Relationships on the
playing field.   ISBN 1-56280-057-4   9.95

KATHLEEN O'DONALD by Penny Hayes. 256 pp. Rose and
Kathleen find each other and employment in 1909 NYC.
                                            ISBN 1-56280-070-1   9.95

STAYING HOME by Elisabeth Nonas. 256 pp. Molly and Alix
want a baby . . . or do they?   ISBN 1-56280-076-0   10.95

TRUE LOVE by Jennifer Fulton. 240 pp. Six lesbians searching
for love in all the "right" places.   ISBN 1-56280-035-3   10.95

KEEPING SECRETS by Penny Mickelbury. 208 pp. 1st Gianna
Maglione Mystery.   ISBN 1-56280-052-3   9.95

THE ROMANTIC NAIAD edited by Katherine V. Forrest &
Barbara Grier. 336 pp. Love stories by Naiad Press authors.
                                            ISBN 1-56280-054-X   14.95

UNDER MY SKIN by Jaye Maiman. 336 pp. 3rd Robin Miller
Mystery.   ISBN 1-56280-049-3.   11.95

CAR POOL by Karin Kallmaker. 272pp. Lesbians on wheels
and then some!   ISBN 1-56280-048-5   10.95

NOT TELLING MOTHER: STORIES FROM A LIFE by Diane
Salvatore. 176 pp. Her 3rd novel.   ISBN 1-56280-044-2   9.95

GOBLIN MARKET by Lauren Wright Douglas. 240pp. 5th Caitlin
Reece Mystery.   ISBN 1-56280-047-7   10.95

LONG GOODBYES by Nikki Baker. 256 pp. 3rd Virginia Kelly
Mystery.   ISBN 1-56280-042-6   9.95

FRIENDS AND LOVERS by Jackie Calhoun. 224 pp. Mid-
western Lesbian lives and loves.   ISBN 1-56280-041-8   11.95

BEHIND CLOSED DOORS by Robbi Sommers. 192 pp. Hot,
erotic short stories.   ISBN 1-56280-039-6   11.95

CLAIRE OF THE MOON by Nicole Conn. 192 pp. See the
movie — read the book!   ISBN 1-56280-038-8   10.95

SILENT HEART by Claire McNab. 192 pp. Exotic Lesbian
romance.   ISBN 1-56280-036-1   10.95

THE SPY IN QUESTION by Amanda Kyle Williams. 256 pp.
4th Madison McGuire Mystery.   ISBN 1-56280-037-X   9.95

SAVING GRACE by Jennifer Fulton. 240 pp. Adventure and
romantic entanglement.   ISBN 1-56280-051-5   10.95

CURIOUS WINE by Katherine V. Forrest. 176 pp. Tenth Anniversary Edition. The most popular contemporary Lesbian love story.

A SINGULAR SPY by Amanda K. Williams. 192 pp. 3rd
Madison McGuire Mystery.   ISBN 1-56280-008-6   8.95

THE END OF APRIL by Penny Sumner. 240 pp. 1st Victoria
Cross Mystery.   ISBN 1-56280-007-8   8.95

KISS AND TELL by Robbi Sommers. 192 pp. Scorching stories
by the author of *Pleasures*.   ISBN 1-56280-005-1   11.95

STILL WATERS by Pat Welch. 208 pp. 2nd Helen Black Mystery.
                                        ISBN 0-941483-97-5   9.95

TO LOVE AGAIN by Evelyn Kennedy. 208 pp. Wildly romantic
love story.   ISBN 0-941483-85-1   11.95

IN THE GAME by Nikki Baker. 192 pp. 1st Virginia Kelly
Mystery.   ISBN 1-56280-004-3   9.95

STRANDED by Camarin Grae. 320 pp. Entertaining, riveting
adventure.   ISBN 0-941483-99-1   9.95

THE DAUGHTERS OF ARTEMIS by Lauren Wright Douglas.
240 pp. 3rd Caitlin Reece Mystery.   ISBN 0-941483-95-9   9.95

CLEARWATER by Catherine Ennis. 176 pp. Romantic secrets
of a small Louisiana town.   ISBN 0-941483-65-7   8.95

THE HALLELUJAH MURDERS by Dorothy Tell. 176 pp. 2nd
Poppy Dillworth Mystery.   ISBN 0-941483-88-6   8.95

SECOND CHANCE by Jackie Calhoun. 256 pp. Contemporary
Lesbian lives and loves.   ISBN 0-941483-93-2   9.95

BENEDICTION by Diane Salvatore. 272 pp. Striking, contemporary romantic novel.   ISBN 0-941483-90-8   11.95

TOUCHWOOD by Karin Kallmaker. 240 pp. Loving, May/
December romance.   ISBN 0-941483-76-2   11.95

COP OUT by Claire McNab. 208 pp. 4th Carol Ashton Mystery.

                                        ISBN 0-941483-84-3   10.95

THE BEVERLY MALIBU by Katherine V. Forrest. 288 pp. 3rd
Kate Delafield Mystery.   ISBN 0-941483-48-7   11.95

THE PROVIDENCE FILE by Amanda Kyle Williams. 256 pp.
2nd Madison McGuire Mystery.   ISBN 0-941483-92-4   8.95

I LEFT MY HEART by Jaye Maiman. 320 pp. 1st Robin Miller
Mystery.   ISBN 0-941483-72-X   11.95

THE PRICE OF SALT by Patricia Highsmith (writing as Claire
Morgan). 288 pp. Classic lesbian novel, first issued in 1952 . . .
acknowledged by its author under her own, very famous, name.
                                        ISBN 1-56280-003-5   10.95

SIDE BY SIDE by Isabel Miller. 256 pp. From beloved author of
Patience and Sarah.   ISBN 0-941483-77-0   10.95

STAYING POWER: LONG TERM LESBIAN COUPLES by
Susan E. Johnson. 352 pp. Joys of coupledom. ISBN 0-941-483-75-4   14.95

SLICK by Camarin Grae. 304 pp. Exotic, erotic adventure.
ISBN 0-941483-74-6   9.95

NINTH LIFE by Lauren Wright Douglas. 256 pp. 2nd Caitlin
Reece Mystery.   ISBN 0-941483-50-9   9.95

PLAYERS by Robbi Sommers. 192 pp. Sizzling, erotic novel.
ISBN 0-941483-73-8   9.95

MURDER AT RED ROOK RANCH by Dorothy Tell. 224 pp.
1st Poppy Dillworth Mystery.   ISBN 0-941483-80-0   8.95

A ROOM FULL OF WOMEN by Elisabeth Nonas. 256 pp.
Contemporary Lesbian lives.   ISBN 0-941483-69-X   9.95

THEME FOR DIVERSE INSTRUMENTS by Jane Rule. 208 pp.
Powerful romantic lesbian stories.   ISBN 0-941483-63-0   8.95

CLUB 12 by Amanda Kyle Williams. 288 pp. Espionage thriller
featuring a lesbian agent!   ISBN 0-941483-64-9   9.95

DEATH DOWN UNDER by Claire McNab. 240 pp. 3rd Carol
Ashton Mystery.   ISBN 0-941483-39-8   10.95

MONTANA FEATHERS by Penny Hayes. 256 pp. Vivian and
Elizabeth find love in frontier Montana.   ISBN 0-941483-61-4   9.95

LIFESTYLES by Jackie Calhoun. 224 pp. Contemporary Lesbian
lives and loves.   ISBN 0-941483-57-6   10.95

MURDER BY THE BOOK by Pat Welch. 256 pp. 1st Helen
Black Mystery.   ISBN 0-941483-59-2   9.95

THERE'S SOMETHING I'VE BEEN MEANING TO TELL YOU
Ed. by Loralee MacPike. 288 pp. Gay men and lesbians coming out
to their children.   ISBN 0-941483-44-4   9.95

LIFTING BELLY by Gertrude Stein. Ed. by Rebecca Mark. 104 pp.
Erotic poetry.   ISBN 0-941483-51-7   10.95

AFTER THE FIRE by Jane Rule. 256 pp. Warm, human novel by
this incomparable author.   ISBN 0-941483-45-2   8.95

PLEASURES by Robbi Sommers. 204 pp. Unprecedented
eroticism.   ISBN 0-941483-49-5   11.95

EDGEWISE by Camarin Grae. 372 pp. Spellbinding
adventure.   ISBN 0-941483-19-3   9.95

FATAL REUNION by Claire McNab. 224 pp. 2nd Carol Ashton
Mystery.   ISBN 0-941483-40-1   10.95

These are just a few of the many Naiad Press titles — we are the oldest and largest lesbian/feminist publishing company in the world. We also offer an enormous selection of lesbian video products. Please request a complete catalog. We offer personal service; we encourage and welcome direct mail orders from individuals who have limited access to bookstores carrying our publications.